The Road to Wainscott

A Memoir

By Frederick Rutledge Smith

ISBN: 1449916279

Frederick Rutledge Smith

Copyright © 2009

Designed by Jordi Waggoner

On the cover, the author in a favorite jacket, Central Park, 1964

This book is for Burton, Ben and Bob

AN INTRODUCTION

I am 84, four score and four. I am in bed by 10 and up at seven. With few aches and pains my good doctors claim that I am on the sunnier side of good health than most "pensione" or retired ones, as the gentle Italians call us politely, instead of "vecchiai," the old ones. My tennis rackets and ski boots are stored in the basement but I go to the local YMCA three times a week and do my cardios, stretches and aerobics. I am a curious and maybe even a good cook and I eat very well.

Of late I find myself lying abed half awake from 6 a.m. to 7. It is reminiscence time. I coast around a lifetime of memories, of people, places and things in a reverie that has become the beginning of my day. The early light, filtering through the solarium that adjoins my bedroom in Wainscott, Long Island, a short way from the Atlantic Ocean, tells me what kind of day waits without. The dogs, Oliver, the beloved aging blond English Spaniel and K-2, the feisty little Lhasa Apso, are waiting for their beginning of the day pee and breakfast.

Sometimes I make mental lists—the 90 places around the globe where I have skied; proud achievements in a 40-year career in publishing; notable characters I have known; cruises and road trips; culinary adventures; life-threatening escapades; first times, great times, tough times. Some of this may be of interest to friends and family, and that is why I am writing this memoir. Its form will be random, but there are things I think are worth recording and tales worth telling.

BEGINNINGS

I was born in 1925, a vintage year. So was The New Yorker. T. S. Eliot published The Hollow Men: *"This is the way the world ends, not with a bang but a whimper."* Scott Fitzgerald published The Great Gatsby, Calvin Coolidge said, "The business of America is business." The first working television set was produced. Sweet Georgia Brown and Dinah were the hit songs and flag-pole sitting was a national fad. An exhibition in Paris called Arts Decoratifs et Industriels launched the style called Art Deco that would create the Normandie, Rockefeller Center and the Chrysler Building.

My parents were good-looking and loving. I arrived in the world on April 5, just 10 months after their marriage in Montgomery, Alabama and their honeymoon on Tybee Island, Georgia. They knew Zelda Sayre, daughter of a local judge and mother's high-school classmate, and Scott Fitzgerald, who met Zelda while based at Maxwell Field army base. Legend has it that my parents, while courting, had double-dated with them. It could have been.

A first memory was of being waked by the noise of dancing and the Victrola playing the Charleston.

3

My honeymooning parents on the beach at Tybee Island, Georgia

My father, Frederick Rutledge Smith, was born in 1899, fifth of six children of Benjamin Bosworth Smith, grandson and namesake of a presiding bishop of the Episcopal Church, and Mary Middleton Rutledge Reese, great great granddaughter of two of the four Charlestonians who signed the Declaration of Independence. I never knew Pop, as my Smith grandfather was called by his children. He died of heart failure when I was only a year old. Pop, born in Louisville, Kentucky, was a Princeton graduate in engineering and architecture. He had been on the team that designed the Louisville and Nashville Depot in Nashville, where he met my grandmother, and moved to Montgomery to design the Union Station, which still stands, now a museum. He also designed Flowers Hall, the Gothic centerpiece of Huntington College, the expansion of the state capitol and some of the finest houses in Montgomery, including a columned structure that is now the governor's mansion.

He was evidently prosperous because he had, in addition to the family house in town, what was for then a rarity, a cottage and land on a lake outside of Montgomery that was called Smith Farm. I have a treasured photograph, taken at the farm in 1921, perhaps of a Sidney Lanier High School graduation picnic. Standing and sitting are about 40 young men and women, all holding slices of watermelon. Pop, with a white shirt and tie, is in the middle.

The girls are in gauzy starched and pressed summer dresses with white stockings. My mother is seated in the front row on the grass, next to a fellow who seems all eyes for her. Perhaps he is Wylie Hill, her first beau. My father is several

Stylishly turned out grandparents, Pop at 6, Mama Smith at 18

rows behind, so this was obviously before they had become close.

Mother was the second of two daughters, born Mary Burton Matthews in 1902 in Huntsville, Alabama, to Lucien Tardy and Clara Burton Matthews. They were grandparents whom I would wish for any child. About 1910 they had moved from Huntsville to Montgomery where my grandfather, Da, would run a 300-acre dairy farm with a fine head of Jersey cows. His father, John Nathaniel Matthews, had been a Confederate soldier and was captured by Morgan's Raiders and imprisoned, coming home at the end of the Civil War to his wife Henrietta Cecilia Tardy, daughter of a Huguenot émigré family, to Mobile and then Huntsville. Before he died of prison-contracted tuberculosis, a young 31, he fathered five children, Da and his four sisters.

I introduce my grandparents here for they were enormously influential on my boyhood and the young lives of my sister, Burton, my brother Ben, and first cousins, Clara, Anne and Harry, children of my mother's sister and her husband, Henrietta and Harry Porter.

When we were all very young, the Smiths lived first on First Street and later on Norman Bridge Road, the Porters on Fairview Avenue, all very close to the dairy, and we spent as much time there as at home. Later, when the Porters moved to Jackson, Mississippi, and the Smiths to

Tuscaloosa when I was 12, we spent our teenage summers and Christmas holidays there.

My cousin Clara, 3, and I at 2 on Da's lap

Life on the farm, called Grielhurst, after the land's owner, Meyer Griel, was a Deep South idyll. As young children, we made our own entertainments, playing cowboys—I was always Hoot Gibson—using the stalls in the cow barn after milking time and the hosing down as our individual forts for shoot-outs. We created theaters in swept dirt under cedar trees, using the tiny blossoms of lantana as ballet dancers. We climbed into the hayloft and slid down hills of hay. Once my sister Burton slid over the side when there was no hay wagon there and landed on the back of a mule, temporarily knocked out but saved from serious injury.

On Confederate Memorial Day, we made wreaths of wire coat hangers and the lavender blossoms of the China berry tree to take to school to be laid on the veterans graves at Magnolia Cemetery. The radio was America's entertainment. Da never missed Amos and Andy or Will Rogers—sacred times for him. On Saturday mornings, the youngsters listened to Nila Mack's Let's Pretend. I can still hear its opening music: Da da dallala, da da dallala, da da dallada. We would often be driven downtown and stop at the Carnegie Library for a week's worth of books to read.

On summer mornings, we rode out with Da before breakfast as he directed the field hands in the beginning of a day of planting or threshing or harvesting oats and sorghum or corn

9

for feed. Coming home, we raced on Tucker, our Welsh pony, or Sport, or the youngest ones, with Da on his Tennessee Walking horse Billy back to the barn and to the kind of breakfast grandmother had waiting, always freshly made hot biscuits, spicy pork sausage or bacon, scrambled eggs and grits. On Sundays, there were waffles or pancakes and Alaga cane syrup, still made right in Montgomery and sold with the motto "The sweetness of the South." The butter was freshly churned from the dairy.

As I write this, I can still taste the wonderful things that came from our Grandmother Matthews' kitchen. She had a wood-fired stove and nearby in a back hall an icebox kept cold by blocks of ice brought to the dairy early before milking every morning. A crank telephone was near it, with multiple subscribers. We were one step removed from living in the Victorian Age.

Grannie claimed to have learned to cook at the side of Aunt Matt, Da's mother's cook in Huntsville. But feeding her family was an act of love. She made batches of penuche and divinity and fruit cakes and plum pudding at Christmas and for each grandchild a favorite birthday cake—mine was Lady Baltimore with white icing filled with pecans and raisins. She rose before dawn to make the hot breads for breakfast. And then later, hoecakes or corn pones, oh my! And for special occasions beaten biscuits, crisp and flakey, pounded with a hand-carved mallet on a biscuit block of granite set into a sturdy table made by Da. There was nothing Paula Dean about her table. I used to earn 10 cents for pounding the dough 300 times before it was rolled out and cut into biscuits and put into the oven to be eaten with country ham from pigs slaughtered on the farm. On Sunday, while the rest of us ate the hot breads she had prepared, Da consoled himself with a slice or two of packaged cottony sandwich bread. His Presbyterian mother had not allowed baking on Sunday, and that remained Da's penance.

On Sunday mornings, I would also crank the ice cream maker, a wooden bucket filled with salted ice surrounding a metal canister of custard to turn into ice cream, vanilla, from the bean not from a bottle, or peaches from the trees behind the house and cream from the dairy that was so rich that it would be half-way down a glass quart of milk that had not been separated. Another dime was nothing as compared to the reward of being allowed to lick the "feather" when the ice cream was freshly frozen.

In season all the vegetables that we ate came from Grannie's garden—turnip greens, English peas, spinach, crowder peas, corn, butter beans and tomatoes. A slice of a beefsteak tomato was the size of a dinner plate. We had chicken every Sunday and many another day too, for Grannie had her own flock of Rhode Island reds. Since there was no chemical fertilizer and all the chickens were free-range, we were pioneers of the organic movement, way back in the 1930s.

Sometimes young chicken, pullets we called them, after the French poulet, would be broiled in a black iron skillet, weighed down by "sad irons." Quail and dove, shot by my grandfather, would also be cooked this way. But the preferred way of cooking chicken was floured and seasoned in a brown paper bag and then fried in lard. My brother Ben hasn't eaten any kind of fowl since he witnessed our grandmother wringing the neck of a hen!

As in every childhood there were traumas, and I had mine as well. When I was six or seven, I was sent for a week at a camp run by Mrs. Walton, my first-grade teacher and her husband, on a lake not far from town, a gift from Da, who was trying to make more of a man of me. I was, I suppose, a bit of a mama's boy, surrounded by a doting mother and a sister and cousins who were girls. My brother Ben was a baby, our cousin Harry not yet born. I hated every moment that I spent at that camp that week. The toilet was in an outhouse in the woods which I refused to visit since I was certain that there were spiders and snakes and bears there. I learned to swim, but water in my ears produced ear ache. I quietly cried my self to sleep on my cot every night.

At week's end, my parents came to collect me with the news that since I had been such a good camper, Da had signed me up for a second week. They said goodbye and drove away with me chasing them, falling on the sandy road in tears.

When I was eight or so I was volunteered by my grandfather to do a bit of work. First chore was to go with the milk wagons with drivers Ben Hall or Will Jones at five or six in the morning on the delivery rounds, mostly around Cloverdale, the upscale part of Montgomery that reached from the Country Club to halfway downtown. I would go to a customer's house on the route to see what was ordered on a note left in a milk basket of empty bottles on a doorstep: milk, eggs, cream, buttermilk, butter. Then back with a filled basket from the horse-drawn wagon.

When I was about 11 my chores became more arduous at a second version of Grielhurst. Meyer Griel had sold the first dairy's land as suburbs began to spread around, making the close-in acres more valuable as real estate than farming or dairying. He bought a large farm with barns, a silo, and a dairy building surrounded by fig trees five miles out of town on the Troy Highway. A new law decreed that all dairy products had to be pasteurized, and the dairy became a wholesale enterprise, delivering its rich milk to a conglomerate, Southern Dairies, instead of Grade A Raw Milk to individual subscribing customers.

13

This was real country with a sprawling house with a big front porch facing a lawn filled with giant pecan trees. It was here that I would work for weeks in the summer in the millet or sorghum fields, cutting millet for silage with a machete, side by side with workers who lived on the place. We were in the fields from six to six, and I recall the pay was $1 a day. I was paid what the hands were paid. It was hard, and hot, but it was also a chance to compete with stronger men than I and to show that I could keep up.

The Negroes never seemed to resent me but were great companions and protectors, killing water moccasin snakes with their blade when they slithered through the cane to the creek .One dollar a day in 1936 may sound like slave wages today, but it was more than many had in that Depression era across the land. Beef steak cost 20 cents a pound, gasoline a nickel a gallon. The workers lived on the place in simple two-room cabins with fireplaces to heat the thin-walled structures in winter and a bit of land for cultivation of chickens and vegetables On Saturdays, wagons pulled by mules would go downtown to Commerce Street taking the men and their women to visit friends and shop for basic necessities.

The most onerous job I had was at threshing time when I was the one who held the gunny sack for the oats. The air

14

was full of chaff that would fly around and stick to the sweat on my neck, and I couldn't let go to scratch the itch without letting the grain spill on the ground. To this very day, I value the growing up experiences of living the farm life, knowing and caring for animals, working with those who tilled the land, having Negroes for mentors and friends.

I deeply regret that I did not know my father's parents and siblings in their halcyon days. The house that Pop had designed for them was a grand old three-storied gabled and shingled structure in the best part of Perry Street, across from the Hills and the Ligons. It was filled with fine antiques—American Empire furniture with carved dolphins and marble tops made in Philadelphia for the Charleston and Tennessee forebears of Mama Smith, our name for her. The accent was on both syllables. At an auction of Andy Warhol's effects, one of the pieces, a dolphin pier table, restored and regilded, sold for $50,000. The family had sold it long after she died for $1,000 to a dealer who claimed he had wanted it for the Mississippi governor's mansion.

There were Belter chairs and settees upholstered in gray cut velvet and great pier-mirrowed credenzas and a fine bronze-ensconced French fauteuil that had belonged, it was claimed, to Josephine Bonaparte. Going up the stairwell and in the dining room were portraits of ancestors including Edward Rutledge, the Signer and Frederick Rutledge,

15

grandson of Edward's brother John, Colonial Governor of South Carolina, a signer of the Constitution, and Chief Justice of the Supreme Court. Frederick was Mama Smith's Charleston grandfather. There was also a portrait of Judge William Brown Reese, her father. In the dining room hung a large standing portrait of sisters with Byronic curls, one in red velvet, the other yellow satin, arms around each other, and head of one on the shoulder of the other. As children, we called them the Long Necked Women. They are Henrietta Middleton Rutledge, who became the wife of her cousin Frederick, and Emma Blake, granddaughters of Edward Rutledge.

That portrait of Frederick, a handsome 25 in 1825 when it was painted, was left first to my father long ago and is now in my home, for his name is the source of our names. My brother Ben, retired Episcopal priest Benjamin Bosworth Smith, after 15 years as rector of Charleston's grand old Grace Church, now lives with his wife Barbara in Mount Pleasant, South Carolina, across the Cooper River from Charleston. He has the sisters' portrait. Ben has served as the chaplain for family reunions, funerals, weddings and other ceremonies at Middleton Place and on the board of Hampton, the grand 1740 columned plantation home of the Horrys and the Rutledges that now belongs to the state of South Carolina.

With the furniture and with the portraits came a great deal of Charleston pride. Even though Mary Middleton Rutledge Reese had been born in Nashville, she never let you forget that she was a Colonial Dame with Charleston ancestry, peppered with such names as Pinckney, Horry, Middleton, Izard, and Rutledge, and that her great grandparents had left Hampton Plantation and Middleton Place to build new lives on large estates in the Tennessee territory. By the time I was old enough to understand and to talk about the past with her, she was living in genteel poverty. She passed a bit of that pride on to me, I must confess, and she would be all aglow if she knew how closely her grandsons, Ben and I, and particularly Ben, many years later renewed kinship with cousin after distant cousin in Charleston.

The financial decline of the Smith family most likely began when Bosworth, my father's eldest brother, was stricken with ptomaine poison while a student at Georgia Military Academy. His fever was so severe that he was brain damaged and he had to be cared for in Bryce Mental Hospital in Tuscaloosa, where he died at 20. The loss of his beautiful first-born son and namesake so depressed Pop that he was never himself again. The death of his first daughter Alice in childbirth soon after added to his reclusiveness.

My father and his brother Carol managed to study business and engineering at the University of Alabama by alternating

17

semesters—one worked while the other was in college, Daddy as a timekeeper for the Atlantic Coastline Railroad. They both belonged to Sigma Nu, and our father was a stellar tenor of the glee club and the business manager of the fraternity, a position which paid for his room and board. Pop died in 1926, but the brothers continued to run the Bosworth Smith Company to build roads and bridges, and even with the stock market crash of 1929 had a modicum of success.

Then came the affair of the Wetumpka Bridge. In 1929, the small firm won the largest contract it would ever have, to build a five-span steel-reinforced concrete arched bridge across the Coosa River in Wetumpka, only miles from Montgomery. It was to replace an old iron bridge at a place in the river just below a meteor crater which had created the Devil's Staircase, an obstacle for river transportation. Wetumpka is Creek Indian for "Running Waters."

Half way through construction, a deluge of heavy rain caused the Coosa River to flood and the Alabama Power Company in Birmingham opened its locks and as an afterthought called down river to tell Wetumpka that water was coming. Uncle Carol, in the construction shack, got the call and rushed to the edge of the river to sound the warning. There were men down in coffer dams who could be engulfed. Fortunately the workmen got out just before the wall of water arrived, but all the substructure--cranes, coffer

18

dams, pilings--of the half-finished bridge, was washed away.

Alabama Power was the state's most powerful utility and its lawyers fought responsibility for the damage to the degree that the case went to the state supreme court. My father, age 31, won the first case ever won against the power company, and a substantial settlement, but the firm never recovered. They completed the Bibb Graves Bridge and it still stands, arching across the Coosa, Wetumpka's most notable landmark. It is one of only two arched concrete bridges in the country and was used by film maker Tim Burton in the recent hit movie Big Fish.

As were most Americans, we were strapped by the Great Depression, though as young children we were barely aware of the stresses it caused our parents Later, as we neared our teens, we became aware of the frugality that hard times demanded and were forever after careful with our own dollars. Uncle Carol and his family moved into Aunt Edith's lovely old pre-Civil War family home in Greensboro, Alabama, and we moved, the five of us, Mother, Daddy, sister Burton, two-year old Ben and I, into the big Perry Street house, occupied only by Mama Smith and her youngest daughter Mary Middleton.

Our move was a temporary necessity, and that was a blessing, for Mother and Mama Smith had a rather formal relationship. I believe that Mother felt that she was looked down upon socially by her autocratic mother-in-law. The perceived slight inspired her to research her own lineage, and she later became a Colonial Dame herself after tracing direct descendency through the Matthews line to Alexander Spottswood, first colonial governor of Virginia.

Aunt Mary had by this time begun a kindergarten for the children of Cloverdale. She turned the music room of the house into the kindergarten room, covering the delicate paintings of cherubs playing musical instruments that decorated the ceiling, portraits of the six Smith offspring as babies, with cartoon images of Mickey Mouse and his friends. I, at the age of five, had been her first pupil. She played the guitar and the piano and we had a rhythm band, triangles and tambourines and drums, and we played kazoos or sang along with her. We also played games that taught us the alphabet and counting and prepared us for the first grade. She was a natural teacher.

After a year, our father had a new job and we were soon in a home of our own once again. Aunt Mary and her mother took in boarders to keep the wolf from the door and food on the table. One of them, Bert Henderson, a handsome gentleman, was the night clerk of the Whitley Hotel. He was also poet laureate of the state of Alabama. He eventually married Aunt Mary, and they stayed on at 1019 South Perry Street for the rest of their lives, a couple out of a Tennessee Williams play. Mary Middleton would not leave her aging mother to live alone.

Daddy had been hired as director of operations for the state of Alabama of the Works Progress Administration, newly elected President Franklin Roosevelt's WPA. His mission was to put as many people to work in newly created and financed federal projects as he could, and he would not leave his office until he had interviewed all who came, lining the halls of his office building, contractors and laborers, carpenters and painters, plumbers and electricians and just plain ordinary hungry people. He often came home after midnight.

He did such a yeoman job of putting people to work that Harry Hopkins, President Roosevelt's right hand man, summoned him to Washington. FDR asked our father how Alabama had performed so well for the WPA. Daddy replied, "Because we were made up of broke, honest contractors, either broke because we were honest or honest because we were broke." While he was there, Hopkins offered our father a directorship of New England's relief programs, and for one brief moment we kids danced with joy at the expectation of a new adventure—moving to

Boston. But our parents decided that we would stay at home in Alabama.

In the three or four years that Daddy was with the WPA he made friends with associates who had formerly been career builders, particularly Lewis Ford and Pat Morrison, who as partners had built much of Mountain Brook, Birmingham's upscale suburb. Lewis Ford, an avid fisherman and golfer, had a cottage on St. Andrews Bay in Panama City, Florida, and as we became close with the entire Ford clan, Lewis, his wife Cynthia, and their daughters Cynthia, Ditsy and Polly, we joined them there for weeks in the summer. Pat Morrison and his family were next door.

Those were really special times at a Florida that no longer exists. There was a sandy path through the palmettos down to St Andrews Bay, our private swimming hole, filled with crab and schools of fish and clearest waters. It was all as unspoiled as a tropical Pacific island. There were excursions in Lewis's cabin cruiser to fish for Spanish mackerel and bonito and drives out for picnics at gulf beaches that were as pristine as when the good Lord made them, not a high rise, not a honky-tonk in sight, just rolling dunes and sand as smooth and as white as talcum powder.

Panama City: Big Cynthia Ford and Mother holding Polly Ford.
In front, Flora Morrison, Ben Smith, Burton, little Cynthia and I

By 1937, the FDR relief programs had begun to take hold and the United States was looking at a more promising future. Daddy, Lewis Ford and Pat Morrison, knowing that government relief programs would not last forever, talked of joining forces in a new endeavor, prefabricated houses, an innovative idea for the time, and to look for a factory to make them. But in the spring of that year, while driving Burton and me to Bellinger Hill School, Daddy said to Burton, "That hurts," when she leaned from the back seat and hugged his chest. That morning after he arrived at his office he had a serious heart attack.

After two weeks in St. Margaret's hospital, he was mandated by his doctors to long bed rest on a diet of milk toast and chicken soup. To give him complete quiet, we three children went to live at Grielhurst for a while. It was a long time, into the 1960s, before medicine had heart patients up and active in a day or two, and such things as bypasses, angioplasties, stents and statin pharmaceuticals were not even on the coronary horizon. That summer, the Smith clan, with Mother driving the entire way, went to Coral Gables to a Florida bungalow that friends loaned us for Daddy's convalescence. The trip took three days, and along with us was our cook and housekeeper Johnnie, who was black. When we stopped for a night in a tourist court, as they were called then instead of motels, we had first to find a place in the black neighborhoods for Johnnie. That was the South of then and a long time afterwards.

TO TUSCALOOSA

By summer's end, Lewis Ford and Pat Morrison had found in Tuscaloosa The Oak City Furniture Company that had closed its doors because of the depression. With a government loan they, with Daddy as a partner, bought the factory, with a saw mill and all its woodworking and lathing machinery, and changed its name to Southeastern Manufacturing Company. We were off to the home of the Crimson Tide. It wasn't Boston, but it was an adventure.

Driving there was part of the adventure itself. The 100-mile road between Montgomery and Tuscaloosa was under construction. For a long stretch we found ourselves on detours, sliding in the red Alabama mud. Daddy, now well and at the wheel, came to a local by the road and asked, "How is the road ahead?" The country fellow said, "Well, t'ain't as bad as it's been a-bein'." This became for us a family expression for any hardship we encountered.

Tuscaloosa was and still is a lovely place, filled with oak trees and antebellum houses. The University of Alabama and the Gulf States Paper Co. were the main employees, the paper mill engulfing the town and tarnishing all silver with its acrid sulfuric perfume when the wind was wrong. We were fortunate to have cousins who lived there, the Cochrane family. They opened doors for us to its old-South society. Mr. Robert Cochrane was the president of the bank. His doctor son, Bob, married to Mother's cousin Lillian, became Daddy's cardiologist. We joined Christ Episcopal Church and in no time at all, Daddy's was not only on the vestry, but also asked to join Rotary. We were not only anointed but accepted.

Moving to a new school, a new community, wasn't easy for me. I was not much of a team-playing athlete. I competed better in the classroom than on the playing field and was not particularly popular with my classmates. Burton, my gregarious sister, made friends that she has to this day. Ben, just entering the first grade, found his niche as well as a continuing roster of sweethearts. Ben was always at every stage in his young life in love. I became a member of the National Honor Society, editor of the class yearbook, and was paraded, by my English teacher, Miss Thames, before the Kiwanis Club as a prize student to give a speech, the subject of which I cannot remember. I do have, however, a copy of a letter written to my father congratulating him on my performance. That kind of recognition was the germ, the seed that caused me, I am certain, to decide years later that my career was in words. I would be a writer, or an editor.

After a year or two in rented houses in Tuscaloosa, our parents built Mother's dream house in a new subdivision developed by the partners in an old cotton field on the periphery of the town. They called it Glendale Gardens. The Fords and the Morrisons also built homes there, and the once treeless farmland was planted with saplings all the way to the end of it. The houses cost, in 1939, $5,000 or $6,000, but they were built by Southeastern craftsmen and with materials obtained at company discounts, everything from plumbing to lumber. The government loan had limited the partners of the firm to salaries of about $3,500 a year. I don't know how I remember these figures but they seemed significant even to a youngster.

Let me pause here and do a computer search for the value of the dollar of then and now in 2009. According to the Templeton Fund, a 1939 dollar is worth about $16 today. That would indicate that one could have built our very comfortable and charming three-bedroom, two-bath house for $90,000 today with the considerable advantage of owning the land and the building company. We also bought a new red Ford V-8 for $950, about $15,000 in today's money. Our annual family income of $3,500 would be $48,000 in today's dollars. In the post-depression South that money would go twice as far in Tuscaloosa as it would have in New England.

An early contract for Southeastern was to build a new country club, replacing a building that had been destroyed by a cyclone, on a golf course with frontage on the Black Warrior River. Partner Lewis Ford was a scratch golfer there, and with the contract to build the clubhouse came family club membership to each of the partners of Southeastern. We were on the road to Easy Street.

But as I said, the memory of hard times was still with us. From the time I was 14, I worked in summer and after school. I had, as had my sister, taken classes in typing and shorthand in junior high school, back up for finding work if work was hard to find. I would ride my bicycle to school and afterward down Queen City Avenue to the office of Southeastern in a house next to the plant.

In 1939, with Europe already at war, my father won government contracts to manufacture prefabricated houses to relocate farmers off of land that would be turned into U.S. military bases and then barracks for army camps at Camp Shelby, Mississippi and Fort McClellan, Alabama. Since we were a company with a government loan and with government contracts, financial reports and payrolls had to be typed on extra wide typewriters to furnish to the government--with a dozen carbon copies of each. My main job was to type them. It did not take me long, once I had erased and corrected mistakes on those forms, to learn how to type numbers and to set and to use the tab keys on that clumsy old Underwood.

Two events stand out in my memory of those days. Before noon on the first Saturday that I began to work there, Miss Effie, the bookkeeper, put the week's pay in cash in marked envelopes, lined up alphabetically in a box, for the 30 or so workers. She asked me to give them to the workmen. I took the box into the factory and went from machine to machine to ask the name of each worker and give him his envelope. Each quickly shut down his machine and vanished. Mr. Snead, the office manager, hearing the factory go quiet came seeking me. No one had told me that the drill was for workmen to come to the office and line up for their pay after the noon whistle sounded. Waiting for them, like buzzards after road kill, as they quickly escaped out the back of the plant, were landlords and grocers and money lenders, hanging around to collect their dole.

The summer that I was 16, I was sent by Southeastern to be the time keeper at a lumber camp near pine lands that the company harvested in Linden, Alabama, a red-clay one-street, one stoplight town, with one movie house that showed a new movie once a week on Friday night. I found a room in a boarding house that was filled with men who were paving a highway near the town. The noon meal—dinner it was called in those Alabama days—cost 25 cents for a family-style abundance of vegetables, corn bread, fried chicken or pork chops, pie and iced tea. From my fellow lodgers I learned that summer a language that I had never heard spoken before, every combination of four-letter nouns, adjectives and verbs that existed and some newly created. Home for a weekend by lumber truck, I had to show off this new vocabulary to my kid brother Ben, now 11, and it was difficult to mind my tongue in general conversation.

Fortunately for the ears of my parents and my sister, I took sick, as they say. I had begun to have severe headaches and in a month lost 10 pounds on an already skinny frame. I had malaria. That was the end of Linden, and I was dosed with quinine and bed bound for the next five weeks.

At the end of that summer, there was consolation, a trip with my father that is one of my most cherished memories. The Mobile and Ohio Railroad had a luxurious yacht based in Mobile that had once belonged to Atwater Kent, a Philadelphian who had made a fortune making radios. The railroad used it to entertain customers and Southeastern shipped timber and prefabs by M&O. My dad, Mr. Blake, our plant manager, and other Tuscaloosa businessmen were asked to board the yacht for four days of fishing in the Gulf of Mexico. Daddy's heart doctor, Bob Cochrane, said that he could go if I went along to monitor him —seeing that he got lots of rest and only one highball per day.

It was the beginning of hurricane season, and a storm had so riled the Gulf that the captain suggested that we, instead of fishing, stay close to ports and sail for New Orleans. We all surmised that he had a girlfriend there. The first night we docked at Biloxi, Mississippi, the next at New Orleans. There were five M&O Pullman car porters aboard to serve us and keep the buffet constantly replenished with shrimp and crab and ham and salads and refill any glass that someone put down. I carefully watched Daddy's glass— Coca Cola and ice except for a bourbon and water before the evening meal. There was a friendly crap game on deck and by the time we got to New Orleans, Daddy had a pocket full of winnings. We docked on Lake Ponchartrain about midnight, too late for a long cab ride to the French Quarter. The crew suggested a nightclub nearby called The Wonder Bar.

As we arrived at the club, we were greeted by statuesque creatures in pancake, lipstick, mascara and rouge, piled up hairdos, tight-fitting panties and bras, mesh stockings and high heels. "So that's what a chorus girl looks like!" I thought. A couple of them came to our table and sat on men's laps and cadged drinks. Then the floor show began: Singing, dancing and then a comedy duo doing an

31

impersonation of one of Bob Hope's radio acts, Brenda and Cobina, named for the most famous debutantes of the New York season, Brenda Frazier and Cobina Wright. "Cobina" kept twirling her pocket book and dropping it. Then as if in anger, she opened the pocket book, took out a long hat pin, stuck it through her left breast and hung the purse on it. "Those aren't girls, they're boys!" Mr. Blake shouted.

The crew members, back at the boat, were doubled in laughter. "How'd you like those drag queens?" they asked, although I think they used a more vulgar term. Next day we went to Maison Blanche on Canal Street to get a present for Mother with Daddy's winnings—a crystal pitcher and julep glasses engraved with MBS. I valued that yacht trip, a teenager among men. It was to be the only time in his life that I was able to share man-to-man experiences with my father.

He had another heart attack that fall and was bedridden on that Sunday afternoon, December 7, 1941, when the news came that the Japanese had bombed Pearl Harbor. We all gathered by the radio at his bedside to hear that America was at war.

I was half way through my senior high school year when I, with four classmates with top grades, was allowed to enter the University of Alabama with the stipulation that we had to pass all courses that first semester to receive our high school diplomas. To get this leg-up on our education in war time, we were encouraged to enroll in what could be classified as militarily significant. The others started pre-med. Daddy recommended chemical engineering as a career for me.

Greek fraternities dominated the campus political, social and intra-mural sports scene and I was flattered beyond belief as I pre-maturely entered college that January. I was rushed and asked to pledge by eight different fraternities, ATO, KA, PhiGam, PiKA, Sigma Chi, Kappa Sig, Deke and Sigma Nu. Of course Daddy hoped that I would become a Sigma Nu, his fraternity, but the members of ATO knew how to charm a green freshman with their blandishments and attentions. They also seemed the most compatible to me and I pledged ATO and never regretted it. The camaraderie and the friendships that I immediately encountered made it a joy to enter college a semester before my high school classmates.

Even during that first semester, I continued to work as a clerk at Southeastern after classes. On an afternoon in May, I was called home from the office. Something was wrong with Daddy. I drove the short distance to our new house in Glendale with my heart in my mouth, and there were three cars in our driveway. Bob Cochrane waiting for me in the living room told me that our father had died. When I entered their bedroom, Mother was with him, cradling his head. He looked as if he were asleep. "What will we do?" I asked through my tears. "We'll manage," she said. Yes, but our world would change.

It was the week of final exams of my first college semester, and the dean allowed me to postpone them. In spite of that, I struggled. A semester of trigonometry, mechanical drawing, physics and chemistry had convinced me that I was not cut out for engineering, as I brought home C's when I was accustomed to A's. Because of the war, the university moved to a quarter system rather than semesters. I joined many others in choosing to go to classes around the year, starting with that summer. But I changed my major to journalism with a minor in English literature.

And indeed, our world did change. Southeastern partners had from the beginning, five years earlier, agreed that should a partner die, the others would buy his shares. It was a moment when the company was on the brink of a massive expansion with army camp contracts, and although Daddy had been the major force in getting those contracts, the value of the company was more in its potential. Our family shares were limited. For years, I would feel, as Mother, widowed at 40, sacrificed to house and educate us, that she had deserved more, as the remaining partners became well to do.

Yes, our father died too young at 42, but he left us with something more than riches. He was a good and principled and much loved man, and he did good things. Mother sold our new house in Glendale, and our new car, abandoned the country club and rented an apartment on University Avenue, across from the A&P, only blocks from the campus. I could walk to class as would Burton and Ben when they were old enough, and Mother could take the bus to work. DeVane Jones, Daddy's lawyer and friend, hired her as a law clerk and typist. With DeVane's advice she invested the settlement from Southeastern in Protective Life, a Birmingham company, and never touched principal, interest or dividends that she received as it grew and shares split until she died, 55 years later, leaving her three children a generous legacy.

With my own well-honed typing skills, I worked afternoons and many an evening for a local entrepreneur, Pettus Randall. He had created "Who's Who Among Students in American Universities and Colleges" and had offices downtown above Lustig's bookstore. He had great success selling books, annual bound listings containing honored students names, as well as certificates and keys to parents and students all across America. He also sent letters to the deans who nominated the students. His success was created by the sincerity of his correspondence.

He used electric typewriters which were operated with player-piano-type rolls that contained letters punched on a device by the office manager. My job, and later my sister Burton's, was to sit on a revolving chair surrounded by four of these typewriters. With envelopes we had already addressed in a stack beside us as guidance, we would type in the date, name and address of students, parents, or the deans, then the Dear Etcetera salutation. Then we would hit the lever and turn to the next machine while the punched out letter was flying through.

About paragraph two, the machine would halt and we would be ready to type in a sincere, "Dear Etcetera," to show it was a personal letter and click the lever and around we would go again. In long letters, that personal touch could happen twice. The pay was $1 an hour. Sometimes, after I typed those things to the tune of more than 60 letters an hour, a letter a minute, until midnight, I could hardly sleep from the stiff back I came home with.

For the 18 months from January, 1942 until June, 1943, I was a happy collegian. I was at ease, now that I had changed to Arts and Sciences instead of Engineering, inspired by my journalism and English lit classes. In Journalism 1, I sat always next to Bebe Montgomery, a Tri-Delt from Birmingham whom I adored. For Journalism 1, we had to read Time Magazine from cover to cover and take tests on even the remotest entry in its pages.

I spent all the between-class leisure time I had at the ATO house which was only two blocks from our apartment. Alabama was known in those days as the Country Club of the South, and the big gymnasium was converted from basketball to a ballroom and stage, jammed for big dances on Saturday night. Every fraternity had an annual ball, with music by a talented local orchestra directed by Tut Yarbrough, to which other frat's boys were asked. We were also on the circuit of the traveling big bands of the swing era—Tommy Dorsey, Vaughan Munroe, Harry James. One scraped for the $10 tickets, wore a tux and danced with girls in silks and satins and gardenia or orchid corsages. When Les Brown played, his cheery blonde songbird, Doris Day, came for lunch at the ATO house. In the presence of the lady who's "Sentimental Journey" was on every jukebox, I was speechless. My first star!

OFF TO THE AIR CORPS

Of course our eyes were always on the war in Europe and in the Pacific as upper class fraternity brothers left for the Army or the Navy. In the spring of 1943 as I neared my 18th birthday, I decided that I would rather join the Air Corps than be drafted into the infantry. If one faced the possibility of death, it seemed more glamorous or glorious in the air than in a trench. There was a primary Air Corps training base across the Black Warrior River in Northport, and British and French airmen had been flying Stearman bi-planes over us for a couple of years.   I went to the base and asked to enlist. After a physical and a psychological exam, I was accepted as a cadet candidate.

My summons came in June, just as I completed my sophomore exams, and I headed for Biloxi, Mississippi, and Keesler Field for basic training. It was a tough 40 days filled with overnight bivouacs, PT--physical training--every early morning, once a week KP, marksmanship practice at the rifle range, and no possibility for leave. It was so summer-Mississippi hot that after long marches and drills, fatigues were white with the salt of our sweat and we would take showers in them to wash them and hang them to dry. Salt tablets came on our mess trays. The upside: I had barracks mates who became close friends for years, particularly Citadel graduate Deuward George Frederick Bultman from Columbia, South Carolina, and a New Orleans native, George Ferdinand von Schminke III. Germanic names like those might have been found in the roster of the Luftwaffe!

For the first year that I was in the service, I wrote home almost every day. I still have all of my letters from those years. I was feeling the responsibility of being the man of the family since our father had died only a year before I left home. Burton was ready to enter the university and Bebe and other of my tri-Delta friends were asking me to encourage her to pledge tri-Delt, to no avail. She became a Kappa Kappa Gamma, an equally prestigious sorority on campus.

The Air Corps was in the process of staffing up. Fleets of training planes and of P-38s, P-47s, B-25s and B-17s were rolling off of assembly lines and training bases were under construction. While we waited in line for flight training, we were sent to Knoxville, for a three-month period of college level classes in history and math at the University of Tennessee and bunked in athletic team quarters in the football stadium. Of course we met local girls. One of them, Polly Galleon, had parents near the campus who were welcoming and generous. Mr. Galleon took the bus to his downtown office to save gas coupons and gave them to us, Polly and two of her friends, dates for Deuward and George, to take a Sunday drive up to Clingman's Dome in the Smoky Mountains at the peak of its fall foliage that October. Nothing was too good for service men!

At last, in January, 1944, six months after we entered the service, we were billeted at Maxwell Field, in Montgomery, Alabama, and officially U.S. Army Air Corps cadets in pre-flight training. We had tough PT each morning, after which we would run in close-order rank for four miles around the base. Then there were classes in Morse code, the principles of aeronautics, weather, map reading and gunnery. There were drill parades for revile and taps and daily spit-and-polish inspections of uniforms and barracks. If a quarter dropped on a tightly, hospital-cornered bunk bed did not bounce three inches high, one got demerits. If brass wasn't polished, shoes shined, footlocker gear neat, one got more demerits. They could earn a careless housekeeper hours of tours, carrying an M-1 rifle.

We were soon fit and disciplined. My friend Deuward, with his Citadel background, was made the cadet commander of our class, 44-J, the J standing for October, the month that we could expect, if all went well, to get our wings. Since Montgomery was second home to me, on the rare weekend leaves we were given I would arrange dates for Deuward and George and also take them to visit my grandparents.

Soon we were off to primary flight training in Albany, Georgia and into the air. In the six weeks there, I learned to fly, and I also edited the class book, a hard-cover publication with pictures of all the cadets of 44-J and of planes and sports teams and base activities. On the frontispiece I used a dramatic photograph of a Stearman PT-17 in cumulous clouds and High Flight, the poem, written by a Canadian RAF pilot, which was an Air Corps mantra:

Oh I have slipped the surly bonds of earth
And danced the skies on laughter-silvered wings.
Sunward I've climbed and joined the tumbling mirth
Of sun-split clouds...and done a hundred things
You have not dreamed of....

That is the way it was. Few things I have done in life were as thrilling as soloing in that sturdy open-cockpit biplane. You have probably heard its put-put-put if you live near an airport, for there are still 1,000 of them around. After the war many were used as crop dusters. On Long Island in summer, one or two of them can be seen above the beaches trailing banners advertising sun lotion or rock concerts. Or you have seen Snoopy's plane in ads and comic strips.

My instructor was a great guy of perhaps 50, Mr. Woodruff, a civilian, as were many primary flying school teachers, under government contract. He was also the chief of instructors, and he had to give check flights to all the junior birdmen in our class. Under his guidance, I soloed in only five hours of flying. Because of his extra duties, he gave the six cadets who were his direct charge more solo time than was customary. "Go on up," he would say, "and practice your stalls and spins."

The Stearman was powered by an eight-cylinder Lycoming engine, a workhorse, a most versatile and easy plane to fly. There were two cockpits, the instructor in the front one, student behind. Communication was one-way by a tube from the instructor to the earlaps of the student's helmet. Make a mistake and the instructor would put his mouthpiece into the wind stream and pop your eardrums. There was a stick rudder to control the ailerons and foot peddles that controlled the tail and pitch and yaw and a throttle to control the power and speed. The instruments were a turn-and-bank horizon indicator, a compass, an altimeter, a fuel gauge, a clock and a speedometer, and that was it. Once I had mastered those controls I would join the others in my class, "shooting stages"—take offs and landings on some farmer's open meadow. We were taught to spin, to loop-the-loop, to fly upside down, hanging from the seat belt, to do snap rolls and barrel rolls and Immelmans as if in a flying circus, or a sky battle with an enemy plane somewhere over Europe.

One of the cadets, Chet Yarbrough, had flown before he entered the service, and he and I would meet at 5,000 feet for dog fights or practicing figure 8's around silos on farms far below. One day he said, "Bet you a Coke I can stay on my back longer than you can." We rendezvoused above a bend in the river and I did a half roll over on my back. In that position, you have to reverse controls, pushing the stick forward to keep the nose above the horizon. The engine conks out after a bit, as the gas won't flow when you are upside down, and you silently coast down, down. I managed a minute or so in that position before doing a half-roll back to normal flight, again powered by the engine. Then Chet rolled over and I watched him from on high as he coasted earthward. When he was precariously low, he did a split-S instead of a half roll. When we were back at the field, we discovered the tip of a pine tree in his left aileron. He won the Coke. By the time we left Albany, I had 60 flying hours, 40 of them solo.

The next stop, basic flying school, in Valdosta, Georgia, wasn't such a cakewalk. The basic trainers, Vultee BT-13s, were closed cockpit with low single wings and tandem seating for two. There were, of course, more sophisticated instruments and controls. You had to change the prop pitch, for instance, for cruising after you powered to altitude. I drew an ornery instructor, a red-headed lieutenant who would much rather have been fighting the Battle of Britain than teaching us tyros. He would bang your knees with the stick and curse you if you didn't follow precisely the things he was trying to teach you. And he failed me on my first check flight.

So as my friends and the rest of my squadron moved ahead, I was assigned remedial flights with a more compatible instructor. After a week, a captain gave me a check ride and after we landed said, "You're fine. Take her up solo." So off I went into the wild blue yonder singing at the top of my lungs the hit from "Oklahoma," "Oh what a beautiful morning, oh what a beautiful day!"

A few days later I was summoned to the office of the commanding officer. He told me that since I was behind my own class, I could be washed back to the one that followed. But then he said that the Air Corps would rather that I should take another course. With the direction that the war was taking bomber crews were in more demand than single-engine fighters, and bombers needed bombardiers and navigators. I had passed the aptitude tests for training as either at Maxwell Field, and the choice could be mine. Losing my buddies, being washed back, made it easier. I have to admit that I was downhearted. Pilot was the glamour job. But I chose, with the guidance of the major, to become a navigator. At least I had danced the skies in my wonderful Stearman.

I was dispatched to Hondo, Texas, a newly built navigation training station 40 miles west of San Antonio. Once again, I was lucky in my bunkmates, two extremely cultivated New Yorkers, Clayton Knight and Fred Boone. Clayton's parents were artists who did New Yorker covers. His brother who lives near me today on Long Island is Hilary Knight, the illustrator famous for creating Eloise, rogue of the Plaza Hotel. Fred Boone had been at Columbia before entering the service and his father was an IBM executive in New York.

As navigation cadets, we were drilled in all sorts of skills, the use of sextants to navigate and plot a course by the stars, by Loran, the newly developed long range radio navigation system, and by dead reckoning, using maps to navigate by objects on the ground. We flew by day, by night, 10 cadets and an instructor in a special training plane, each with a desk and instruments. We had to calculate ground speeds, drift and wind direction, and estimate times of arrival at target and home bases. We would be roused at various hours of the night to learn to identify the major stars and constellations used by navigators since Ulysses.

On a weekend trip to San Antonio, my Yankee roommates introduced me, in one memorable dinner at the St. Anthony Hotel, to my first martini, my first artichoke. With them, I listened to the Metropolitan Opera broadcasts on Saturday afternoons at the cadet club and to the New York Philharmonic on Sundays. We talked endlessly about the future, and they were both at Penn Station to greet me four years later when I arrived on The Southerner to start my New York career.

We were awarded navigator wings in January, 1945, and officer uniforms, flight hats and second lieutenant bars. I had been in the Air Corps for 18 months. I was sent to Avon Park, Florida, to become a navigator on a B-17, the famous four-engine, high-tailed Flying Fortress. Once again, I was lucky. I was a member of Crew 55, the best crew on the base, with Jesse Washburn, former University of West By God Virginia quarterback as our pilot. He had a white Harley, bought from the Minneapolis police department, which he carried in our bomb bay on training missions so that wherever we landed he always had wheels for the chase. He carried a bottle of bourbon in one saddle bag, a blanket in another. Jesse was a terrific leader and pilot, and a world-class ladies man.

B-17 Crew 55 at Avon Park, with our parachutes and life vests.

We flew every day. Every member of the crew had to learn to use the 50-cal machine guns that were fore and aft and on the sides. The B-17 was not pressurized and even in Florida we wore fleece-lined leather flight suits and oxygen masks because of the cold thin air at altitudes above 10,000 feet. Fighter planes were dispatched to attack us, and we tracked them with movie cameras on the guns instead of with ammunition. Flying at about 500 feet we used live ammunition at targets on the ground—strafing houses and signs the Air Corps had built in the Everglades to simulate towns. Once we bombed Boston—photographically. My task was to navigate from Florida to a turning point at the tip of Cape Cod and head for Boston. Then John Westfall, our bombardier in the nose of the plane, took over to pin point the city.

We were named the first Crew of the Week, which meant that we could take an RON, a remain-over-night, anywhere we wanted to go. The nine of us chose New York. We had to take off at midnight and return by midnight of the second night.   Landing at Mitchell Field on Long Island at dawn, we took the train to Penn Station and checked into the Pennsylvania Hotel for a couple of hours of sleep before touring such high spots as Rockefeller Center and Times Square.

That night we went to Billy Rose's Diamond Horseshoe in Times Square for dinner and a floor show of long-limbed scarcely clothed dancers and after, to beat the 11 p.m. curfew, walked down a darkened Seventh Avenue to the hotel. As we headed for the elevators, we heard music in the Café Rouge, the hotel's famous night club, and peeked in. Jimmy Dorsey and his orchestra were rehearsing. "Come in boys," Jimmy Dorsey called. They had Scotch and glasses and ice and offered us drinks. We had our own private party as Bob Eberle and Helen O'Connell sang "Green Eyes" and "Amapola" and "Tangerine." Our flight engineer, Bill McMichael, had a fine voice himself, and the next day as we flew back to Florida, sang those Dorsey hits, music that we had loved and danced to in college, on the plane's intercom.

As we completed our training, we were slated to ferry a B-17 to England as members of the 8th Air Force. The week before we were to leave Avon Park, the war in Europe ended on May 8, 1945. VE Day was, of course, for all America, for all the free world, a glorious and happy day, but for our crew there was a letdown, not getting to Europe and the action that we had been training for.

We were off to Gulfport, Mississippi to crew B-29s, the Boeing Superfortress, designed to fly much higher, to 40,000 feet, and further, 5,000 miles, than the Flying Fortress. It could cross the Pacific where the war still raged. The transition wasn't difficult for a crew trained in the B-17. The B-29 cabin was pressurized and the space more comfortable for all of us. On the first of August, we were dispatched to Kearney, Nebraska, a staging base, waiting for our Pacific assignment. There we listened, on August 6, to the news of the dropping of the atomic bomb on Hiroshima by the B-29 Enola Gay. On August 9, the second bomb was dropped on Nagasaki. We left Kearney by troop train for San Francisco on August 12. Our mission: Guam.

The first night, the train stopped at Cheyenne to take on fuel and water and we had a half hour to rush to the nearest saloon. The bar tender at a long bar, lined with cowboys, said, "Stand back, drinks are on the house for the boys." We crossed the great American desert all the next day and the High Sierra of California at night. When we arrived at Oakland we were put on ferries—the Oakland Bridge had not been built—to the Ferry Building at the foot of Market Street in San Francisco. It was there that we were told by the officer who greeted us that that day, August 14, was indeed V-J Day. We were bussed to a tent village out by the airport and informed that flights overseas were cancelled and that we could go to the city.

Market Street was awash with celebrating civilians, soldiers and sailors and the wild and unruly mob was breaking all the store windows on the street and throwing merchandise to the crowd. There were people making love in the middle of the street. There were even rapes. A couple of WACs asked us to protect them, and we headed up Nob Hill to the Top of the Mark, the famous bar atop the Mark Hopkins Hotel. That's where we celebrated the end of World War II. Our crew was billeted, not in a tent, but for the next two weeks at the St. Francis Hotel. What a way to end a war, in beautiful and salubrious San Francisco! It was easy to fall in love with the town and I returned whenever I could in the years to come.

Our crew was sent to March Field in Riverside, 50 miles from Los Angeles. We continued to fly to get in flight time and receive flight pay. But this was not training for war. We

50

even flew a sewing machine to Denver for the wife of a general. And we hitchhiked on weekends to Los Angeles. The USO in the Biltmore downtown would find us rooms in YMCAs or private homes and tickets to the live Sunday afternoon broadcasts in Hollywood of Bob Hope and Jack Benny.

Home safe in Tuscaloosa, with Mother, Burton and Ben

We were offered a chance to stay in the Air Corps if we would sign up for reconnaissance duty mapping Japan. But I declined that tempting opportunity and headed home in January, 1946.

I had been ready to fight, even die, for my country, and my country was certainly generous to me. I had toured it, by train and by plane, from the tip of Florida to Cape Cod, from Texas to California. I had learned to map the stars, to fly upside down and right side up, the Morse code, to fire M1 rifles and 50-cal machine guns. I had made friends from all corners of America, had savored a Texas martini and abalone from the depths of Monterey. I was fitter than ever in life and not even 21. And I was about to finish college on the GI Bill.

TO BECOME AN EDITOR

Back in Tuscaloosa, the university had a different tone. The student body was more mature, more serious than it had been in my teen days, as returning GIs, many of them married with beginning families, swelled the class roles. During the time in the service I had become directed. I now knew what I wanted to do in life. I had been a good student before, but I became more career oriented than grade oriented. My journalism classes seemed aimed at careers on Southern newspapers or radio stations. I wanted to edit books or magazines.

Looking for experiences that would lead me up the publishing ladder, I answered an ad in The Saturday Review: "Writer for the slicks needs assistant for the summer. Must have driver's license and be a good typist. Send resume and photo." I answered and John Maloney of Silver Springs, Florida, wrote, offering me the job. He was a regular contributor to Collier's and The Saturday Evening Post. I would be paid room and board and all expenses and $100 a month. I had been selected from 500 applicants.

What a summer! John had a cottage with a screened sleeping porch on the banks of Silver Springs, a tourist attraction near Ocala, famous for its crystal water, water-skiing shows and glass bottomed boats. He had had a heart attack and his doctor forbade him to drive alone. When I arrived in June I found a film crew in residence making The Yearling on the site, with Gregory Peck, Jane Wyman, and young Claude Jarman as Jody Baxter. John had worked on the script during the beginning of the shooting and we were allowed to go to the set in the nearby palmetto-filled pine forest and watch the filming of Jody with his fawn.

John was a friend of Marjorie Kinnan Rawlings, who had written the immensely popular best seller, The Yearling, from which the movie was being made. We went weekly to her house in Cross Creek for her special daiquiris and wonderful meals of smothered chicken or fried fish. Miss Rawlings was a fabulous cook and soon published another best-selling book, Cross Creek Cookery. Over the summer, I drove John the length of Florida as he did stories on Seminole Indians and on buried pirate treasure and then helped with the research and typed the manuscripts.

The herpetologist Ross Allen had a rattle-snake farm as part of the Silver Springs attraction, and people came to watch him milk the snakes into vials for anti-snakebite serum. Local Seminoles supplied him with snakes, as well as frogs to feed the snakes. When frogs were too big for a snake to swallow, Allen would give us the frog's legs which I learned to dip in corn meal and sauté in lard. There was also a zoo filled with young deer that had been used in the movie. Fawns changed their spots so quickly as they grew that Seminoles had to supply Clarence Brown, the director, with ever changing editions of Flag, the fawn in the movie.

Of all my English lit courses, the most riveting was the one taught by the most celebrated boulevardier of a professor on the campus, Hudson Strode. Dr. Strode—I still think of him as Hudson--had acted on Broadway while a student at Columbia. With his trimmed mustache and rakish fedora, he looked like Adolph Menjou of the movies and acted, not read, Shakespeare's plays to his students, taking every role. I was an enchanted and a dedicated student, and the following semester he asked if I would be the grader for his Shakespeare classes.

This led to more. He also taught a nationally known class in creative writing, taking only 12 students a semester. From grading Shakespeare, I became a member of the class with a roll of reading the submissions of the hundreds of applicants from all over the South. I was soon his driver and his friend. He and Therese, his stylish and devoted wife, had a modern house surrounded by dogwood trees decorated with Swedish modern furniture, some of which had been in the Swedish Pavilion of the 1939 World's Fair. His students had published many first novels and he knew all the New York

55

book publishers. He wrote a book every other year, most of them travelogues on Scandinavia, Mexico, Bermuda and the Far East, and also a two-volume biography of Jefferson Davis. He also collected famous faces, and persuaded such notable writers as Nobel Prize winners Sigrid Undset and Sinclair Lewis to come and stay in the Strode guest house and lecture at the university. I was often invited to tea when a famous face was in residence.

The university had given me course credits for the time I had been in the Air Corps—all my math and science requirements, for example--and I soon had my BA. I had New York publishing as a goal and feared that job seekers from Ivy League schools would have advantages over this U of A graduate. I also felt the need of a better grounding in culture and decided to add the carnet of a Master's in English. The dean offered me a fellowship teaching Freshman English if I would stay. I could enhance a resume with a Master's and earn a bit of money to fund my next step.

OFF TO NEW YORK

In June, 1948, I was ready to spread my career wings. Brother Ben had entered the university as a journalism major and he pledged ATO even before he graduated from high school. I guess my big brother influence still worked. Burton had graduated and was going to the University of Tennessee to graduate school. Mother was still working in DeVane Jones' law office. When they took me to the station to catch the Southerner to New York, Mother gave me a lovely gift. "I hope you don't come home unless you want to," she said, her version of "break a leg."

I had a new suit and $500 which I had saved from my various endeavors. I had letters from Brooks Forehand, head of the English department, claiming I was a Phi Beta Kappa and from Hudson Strode. I wasn't a Phi Beta Kappa, even though my graduate school grades were straight A's. The credits that I got for my Air Corps days were credited as C's. But Hudson's letters addressed to leading lights of the publishing world were terrific door openers.

Fred Boone and Clayton Knight, my old Hondo roommates, met my train and took me to a small hotel in Greenwich Village and to Clayton's parents on West 9th Street for dinner. With their advice, I searched the pages of The Villager for apartments to rent. Friends from school, Charlie McBurney, John Orr and Rusty McDavid were also job hunting. We teamed up and leased a two-bedroom cold-water flat on west Charles Street above a fire house for $80 a month and started making our job-searching rounds.

In my second week in New York, Miss Amy Loveman, doyenne of the book publishing world, an editor on The Saturday Review and a member of the board of the Book of the Month Club, invited me to a Sunday brunch in her apartment. She was a friend of Hudson Strode's and regularly entertained young people in publishing. The following day she called and asked "Mr. Smith, how would you like to be one of the Book of the Month's freelance readers? It will help tide you over." The BOMC was very powerful back then and every publisher sent them galleys of books they were publishing. The BOMC had every one of them vetted. In the next two years, I read 200 would-be-candidates and wrote an evaluation and a synopsis of each of them. I was paid $7.50 for each report, and if asked to write a review for the Saturday Review, another $15. I learned to read rapidly—two hours to page through, another hour to write my report. The money made the difference between living and existing, and the fact that I was a BOM reader was an invaluable item on my resume. So were the facts that I could type, knew shorthand, and had worked since I was fourteen.

In the four weeks from June 15 to July 15 I had 40 job interviews, something that no one looking for a position in publishing would be able to do today. Three years after the end of World War II, companies were staffing up. I used Hudson's contacts in the book world but book publishers, interviewing a Southerner, had but one job to offer, that of college traveler to help sell text books on southern college campuses. I was told by such important chief editors as Marshall Best of Viking, John Selby of Rhinehart, and Bill Raney of Holt, that this was the avenue to eventually becoming an editor. But I wanted to start where the action was, in New York and editing, not selling.

So I concentrated on magazines. I had a system. When Brendan Gill of The New Yorker said that there was nothing there for me, I asked him whom I should see. "My friend Bob Coughlin at Life," he said. "May I use your name," I asked, and he said, "But of course." I would rush downstairs, put a nickel in the phone and call Bob Coughlin and say that Brendan Gill had recommended me. In every case, the friendly folks in publishing would say, "Come on over." I had three or four interviews a day and spent my evenings typing resumes.

Life, the most successful magazine in the country, offered me a job and I turned it down, my third week in New York. It is hard to believe, but it was as a photo researcher, and I feared that that was too far away from the word. I will never know if that was a stupid decision. Then Andree Vilas, managing editor of Charm Magazine, "the magazine for the BG," or business girl, a sister publication of Mademoiselle at Street and Smith, offered me a job as her assistant. She would teach me magazine publishing, she said, and I was hooked. The salary was $40 a week. But a subway ride cost a nickel as did a pay phone in those days, and my share of the apartment rent was only $20 a month. Every Friday Miss Vilas would have me cash a check for her in the bank downstairs for $100, and I wondered how anyone could possibly spend that much on living in a week.

Charm had a theater critic, Oliver Claxton. Reviewing for a monthly publication, he received second-night press tickets to theater openings. If the daily press panned a show on opening night, he would offer me his tickets, and in the year I was at Charm I saw about 40 Broadway clinkers, and, by sitting in the balcony or standing, such hits as Oklahoma, Mister Roberts and The Member of the Wedding with Julie Harris and Ethel Waters.

My roommates and I had a BYOB party almost every Saturday night and other Alabamans would come. We called ourselves The Albanians. Among them was Nell Harper Lee who had been the editor of the magazine Rammer Jammer at the university and in journalism classes with me. She was busy writing a book that was to become To Kill a Mockingbird.

A fraternity brother, Gordon Clark, arrived in New York and bunked in with us on Charles Street. He found a job as a page at NBC and thought he was going to be a star in the new world of TV. Charles Street was too crowded and together, through a book editor friend, Don Elder, we found a small apartment at 328 East 53rd Street. But Gordon was harder up for cash than he had admitted and gave me IOUs while I carried more than my half of the rent on the new apartment than I had expected when we signed a lease.

Then, fortunately, along came the Pyramid Club. This was a scheme, not unlike a Ponzi scheme in investing, where one and a friend would join 10 others at someone's apartment and each new member would give $2 to the host who would take the money to the name on the top of a list. Each day one would move up the pyramid while others joined below. The potential payoff when you reached the top of the heap, 10 days after you joined, was $2,048. This scheme had started in the Seventh Avenue garment district and the fashion girls at Charm were in on the second or third day and roped me in.

61

The trouble with this pyramid scheme is that it would take the entire population of Manhattan to keep it going for a month, taking two to the progression of 30. New joiners, frantic to keep the pyramid from decaying below them, tied up New York's telephones so completely that business stopped in its tracks that April. But I was in early enough to get a payoff. On the night I reached the top, the buzzer downstairs rang continually from 6 until almost midnight. I had to get Camille Maxwell and Margaret Price, Tuscaloosa girls who lived on the floor above, to come and help me. The entire cast of Make Mine Manhattan came. Gypsy Rose Lee came, all giving me sacks of money. I filled the bath tub with dollar bills! My payoff was $1800. Gordon and I took Camille and Margaret across the street to Louise Junior's famous Italian restaurant at midnight, the first restaurant meal I had been able to afford in a while. And the next day I got my shirts out of the laundry next door and deposited the rest of the cash in my bank account. Pyramids are illegal, but winning one when you are almost broke is a joy!

Andree Villas taught me how to put a magazine together, but after a year, I realized that Charm with its pages of women's fashion was not a place where I could climb the masthead. An employment agent sent me over to True, The Man's Magazine for an interview, and I was hired as an assistant editor at the exalted salary of $65 a week. True, published by Fawcett, had a circulation of 3,500,000 and was enormously successful. It had as its terrific editor Ken Purdy who was a sports car nut and wrote books about car racing.

I seemed to have a particular knack for writing heads and decks to accompany the beautifully illustrated features of the magazine. Examples that I remember: a story about Pinkerton, the detective: "Peekaboo Pinkerton, Private Eye." Or Evelyn Nesbitt, the paramour of Stanford White, "The Girl in the Red Velvet Swing." A movie was made using that title. Soon Ken Purdy had all the editors send me their articles to write the heads and decks. Before long I was put in charge of buying the 10-to-15 thousand-word abridged book feature, the long read that was the last story in the magazine each month.

My biggest coup was persuading Polly Adler, once New York's most famous madam, to sell me condensation rights to her risqué memoir, A House Is Not a Home. Billed on the cover, it raised newsstand sales that month by 250,000 copies and Fawcett gave a press party at 21 for me and Madame Adler. I have a photo of the two of us sitting side by side with the magazine in front of us in the Remington Room of that famous club. I was promoted to associate editor of the magazine.

Madame Adler and I at True's party at the 21 Club

True had a men's fashion feature and the son of a Baltimore haberdasher was hired to edit its pages which brought in advertising from the shoe, the apparel and the luggage industries. The editor knew the market he was covering but he couldn't write his way out of a paper bag, and I was asked to edit his copy. He quit and Ken Purdy asked me to produce the menswear pages. I agreed to do so for a raise and the chance to keep my other responsibilities, such as buying that back of book feature. I did not want to be typed as a fashion editor. But I did produce some imaginative articles. For one called How to Pack a Two-Suiter, I had Samsonite make a suitcase with one side of clear plastic instead of leather. We photographed a model holding it as he boarded an American Airlines plane with his wardrobe showing through. This led into spreads of photo-demonstration on how to pack. For one called If the Shoe Fits, I had Johnson and Murphy cut a Blucher in half from toe to heel for a double-page photo that showed what was inside a good shoe.

I went back to Tuscaloosa at least once a year. Once, in 1950, wearing Daddy's white tie and tails, I gave away my sister Burton when she married Henry Harris, a Tuscaloosa native who had moved to Louisville to help run his uncle's wholesale paper company. The Cochrane family once again proved how supportive they were by hosting the reception in their antebellum home.

Next I went back to Tuscaloosa for Mother's marriage in 1951 to Henry Hale, a banker and family friend who had lost his wife. For the decade since our father's death, she had dedicated herself to getting her three offspring through college, never accepting an invitation to have lunch or dinner with a would-be suitor. She was still and was to the end of her life, a very attractive woman. The whole town was abuzz when she was seen walking down Greensboro Avenue hand in hand with Henry Hale. They spent the next four decades touring the South, winning bridge tournaments, and taking European tours and cruises,

And my social life was looking up. I had a new apartment at 44 East 65 Street and a new roommate, Ed Stackhouse, a friend who worked at the advertising agency, BBDO. He was a Williams College graduate and was dating Katrina Hickox, daughter of Catherine Barker Hickox, heir to the Pullman Railroad fortune. I dated her Bennett college roommate, Lucy Blount, whose father was CEO of Liggett and Meyers Tobacco Company. The Hickox family had a triplex apartment at 10 Gracie Square, filled with European master paintings—Titian's Danae and a Van Dyke in the living room, for example, and Cezannes in the bedrooms--and a large estate at Old Westbury Long Island with a stable full of hunters. Charles Hickox was master of the Meadowbrook hounds.

We would be invited for deb parties and weekends and go beagling on the nearby Jock Whitney estate. They had a tack room with jodhpurs and boots to fit any guest. We learned to clear fences as we rode—low ones, of course. My farm boy experience in the saddle was a boon. Once we went in the Hickox's chauffeured Rolls Royce to the Army Navy game in Philadelphia and often, with Mr. and Mrs. Hickox, to the Metropolitan Opera on Monday—black tie night. Several times I took Lucy to the Stork Club where there was never a check. Sherman Billingsly its proprietor liked to paper the room with young attractive post-debs.

Lucy Blount and I at the Stork Club

Ed Stackhouse was drafted into the Army as the Korean War was upon us and I didn't feel comfortable carrying the apartment rent by myself so I moved to a ground-floor-through of a Greenwich Village town house at the corner of West 4th Street and West 11th Street—there is such a curious address. I shared it with a fraternity brother from Tuscaloosa, Sam Bealle, who was a student at Parsons School of Design. He was also waiting tables at night at The Lion, a popular village restaurant.

Timing in life is sometimes everything and living in The Village in those days was pure delight. It was very much like a small town surrounded by a metropolis, walkable, inexpensive, friendly. You got to know all the shop keepers and your neighbors. None of today's excesses, the high rents, the apartment towers and the louche life had taken over. It was as it had been in the earlier part of the 20th Century, an artist and writer haven. Edna St. Vincent Millay's very narrow house was two doors down the street.

I kept my eye on publishing start ups, and they were everywhere. There were failures, too, many of them, and I was wary of anything that would be fly-by-night. The Reader's Digest Company, with a magazine that had the largest circulation in America, was beginning its Condensed Digest Books Division and a friend at the Digest suggested I might look into their staffing. Through his help I was granted—and that's the proper verb—an interview with Lila Wallace, co-founder of the Digest with her husband DeWitt. In addition to her country club like headquarters in Pleasantville, New York, she had a suite of offices at the top of the Grand Central Building. I recall a décor that was all rose and pink, and Mrs. Wallace wearing pink tweed, a pink jersey turban and tourmaline rings. She sat beside me on a pink settee and said, "Since you are from the South, I suppose that you are either a Baptist or an Episcopalian. And I also imagine that you are a Democrat," as she put her hand on my knee. Alabama was strongly Democrat politically in those days and I admitted to being Episcopalian and Democrat.

The next day I was interviewed by her husband DeWitt over coffee as he finished lunch at the Barclay Hotel. He was a quiet, even taciturn man, and I did most of the talking. I was soon summoned to Pleasantville to be interviewed by Ralph Henderson, chief editor, and not long afterwards offered a job at almost twice my salary. Mrs. Wallace had told me that should I join the Digest company, it would be best to live in White Plains, a larger town than Pleasantville, since it would be more amusing for a bachelor. The company would pay for my move and see that I was admitted to any club of choice. The Digest was notably paternalistic, too much so for my taste. And besides, New York was my Apple, and I declined the offer.

Later, the friend who had started all of this called me to say, "I am surprised that you were offered an editorship. The table of organization called for the next hire to be a Midwestern Jew!" Political correctness was not yet a mindset! I am glad that I met the Wallaces. They had no children of their own, and they left a substantial legacy to the public good, supporting Public Television, the Metropolitan Opera and the Metropolitan Museum. When I go to the Met and see the display of flowers in the great reception hall, a Lila Atchison Wallace bequest, I think of her all in pink.

SPORTS ILLUSTRATED AT LAST

In the spring of 1954, the word was around that Time-Life was planning a new weekly, a sports and leisure magazine. Time, the nation's major news magazine, was created in 1924. Then had come Fortune, in 1933, as America crawled out of the depression, and Life in 1936, the most successful magazine launch of the century. This would be the first publication that Henry Luce would introduce after World War II. I had been at True five years and had gone as far as I could go so I started my campaign at Time-Life. I had been told that they were looking for a fashion editor, and maybe, after all, that part of my True experience could be useful. Friends at Fawcett knew people involved, and I put together a resume and loose-leaf book of my editorial achievements and sent it to the top edit secretary.

There were 5,000 applicants for positions at the new magazine, with many being filled by in-house writers and reporters moved over from Time and Life. They were only hiring about 30 art and editorial staffers from outside the company. I got an interview, first with Dick Johnston, assistant managing editor, and he passed me on to Sidney James, the Life man who was to be Managing Editor. (That was the title of all of Luce's top dogs. Only Luce was Editor-in-Chief.)

On June 15, 1954, Sid James hired me as a staff writer for the department that would be called Sporting Look at the as-yet- unnamed magazine at almost twice the salary I was being paid at True. This turned out to be a life-changing event and it came at a most propitious time. Fawcett was being badly managed. Its owners, the Fawcett brothers, were profligates, spending profits on country clubs and Greenwich estates and extravagant safaris to Africa and fishing expeditions to Canada. That very week the company had announced a 10-per-cent salary cut for all staffers. I went from Sid James' office directly to a pay telephone downstairs in the Time-Life building and called Ralph Daigh, editorial director of Fawcett, and gave him my notice. "Keep the salary cut. I have a new job." Ken Purdy said to me the next day when I went to tell him goodbye and pick up my things, "Well, everyone needs to work for once in his life with all the facilities. Good luck to you." He knew what he was talking about. His sister was an editor at Time. A month later, he and the entire editorial staff of True left Fawcett and took over the editorship of its big competitor, Argosy. Sic transit Gloria mundi.

The next week, my brother Ben, recently graduated from Virginia Theological Seminary, was to be ordained as an

Episcopal priest. I took the train to Tuscaloosa to celebrate, to witness, to photograph the moving event at Canterbury Chapel on the U of A campus, when that magnificent man of a bishop, Charles C. J. Carpenter, laid his large hands on my brother's head. It was June 24, St John the Baptist Day. By an uncanny coincidence, it was on the very same day a century before that our great-great grandfather, Benjamin Bosworth Smith, also age 24, became a priest.

Bishop CCJ Carpenter ordains my brother Ben

He is the ancestral source of Ben's name and was to become the first Bishop of Kentucky and the presiding bishop of the Episcopal Church in America. I like to think that my leaving home helped Ben find his own life's path; discovering that it was not journalism but the church that was his calling. He, in his maturity, with no father figure but me, no longer felt the need to emulate his big brother Fred. He became his own man. He describes his journey in his memoir, My Own Story, far better than I can. He published it earlier this year, 2009, and now, that he is not only my brother but Father Ben inspires me to write this memoir of my own.

The "and then I wrote" form of this odyssey so far will, I trust, be of interest and perhaps value to young readers, particularly my great nieces and nephews. One of the greatest gifts I had growing up was to know, even as a teenager, what I wanted to become as an adult and set my goals to get there by every means I could think of. I tailored my schooling to prepare me to become a writer and an editor. And once I was on that road, I turned down temptations that seemed to branch in other directions. My new job at Time-Life was the felicitous pay-off. I was at last financially secure and soon moved to an apartment at 400 East 57th Street, a block from Sutton Place, and lived there for the next 40 years.

That first summer, the new staff of the magazine which did not yet have a name began to formulate it and to practice meeting weekly deadlines with copy. A dummy of the magazine bore the title MNORX, five meaningless letters which undoubtedly were meant to translate to SPORT. After all, the Luce publications were Time, Fortune, Life. What else?   The trouble was that McFadden already had a magazine called Sport. As the price offered to sell Luce that title went to the stratosphere, a reputed $200,000, we became Sports Illustrated. In July, we produced, under weekly-deadline, dry runs for the real thing. The first live, for real issue of the magazine was published on August 14, 1954.

From the very first issue until many years later, Sports Illustrated was a magazine with a publishing mission that one would not recognize today. Henry Luce, in his methodical way, had begun to search for the next magazine in his empire, almost 20 years after his mega launch of Life. World War II had changed America. He created The Greenwich Study, a deeply researched door-to-door look at the households of that upscale Connecticut community only an hour from New York, home to most of Madison Avenue's taste makers. What did America want?

The study called for a magazine dedicated to The New American Leisure, sparked by the changing pattern of work itself, with two-day weekends for all, disposable incomes and lots of time off for play. The research called for a magazine that would appeal to a country club set, aimed at dual audiences, male and female, with a taste for the fun of playing as well as the joy of watching the game, one that advertisers of travel, fashion, food, cars, the good life, would support. Those first dummy issues we produced were larded with advertising that came from the pages of such successful publications as The New Yorker, Holiday, and House and Garden, Television, in its black-and-white infancy, had not yet brought sports events into every home, and spectator sport had not taken over the networks.

The magazine had also hired a fashion associate to work with me, Jo Ahern Zill, who had been the sportswear editor of Women's Wear Daily. The two of us produced 39 different stories in the first year of the magazine, ranging from sports car racing gear in California to top hats at a horse show first night at Madison Square Garden, Alpine climbing knickers in Zermatt, Scandinavian-inspired ski clothes in Aspen, Tommy Bolt's alpaca golf sweater, Mrs. William Woodward in a Mainbocher suit at the Belmont Stakes. Vic Seixas, U.S. men's single tennis champion at Forest Hills, wore a plaid cashmere sport jacket in a story on the origin of the sport jacket. Some of the stories were filed by famous photographers most notably by socially well-connected Toni Frissell who had worked for Vogue.

*First issue of SI launch party, with designer Claire McCardell,
Fashion Editor Jo Zill is just behind.*

We were not using models, but those we thought of as "real people" and Toni captured them in Europe and Palm Beach and fancy sports events on Long Island.

In its first year the magazine also covered 95 different sports, including in its very first issue, Roger Bannister's defeating John Landry in the under-four-minute mile, the Mile of the Century. The writing and the photography was exemplary from the start. In addition to the talented staff of writers and reporters, we had bylines by William Faulkner and John Steinbeck, Budd Shulberg and Paul Gallico. We were influenced by the pictorial power of Life and, with ex-Lifers at the helm, it is easy to see why. We were also initiated into the scrupulous Time Magazine checking system that let no name, no date, no fact go unchallenged until proved valid. No carelessness of maybe it was like this, or they said it was like that.

Most of the staff writers, covering the major sports events of the week, wrote their stories and let a picture editor and an art editor decide how they would look on the page. I had learned that grabbing a reader with a compelling head and graphic, would get them into a story. I thought visually, as I had been trained to at True. From the beginning our pieces were pictorial. I wanted to go out, to travel and find stories.

I was sent to the upscale suburb of Chicago, Oak Park, Illinois to cover a fancy hunt ball that fall. The gentlemen were in their hunting-pink tails, the women in silks and jewels. After the cocktail hour, when we had enough film, Mrs. Armour, chairlady of the event, said to Jerry Cooke, the photographer and to me, both in black tie, that she had seats for us for dinner at a table with the help in the kitchen. The help! We were Time-Life! Jerry opened his Nikons and unrolled canisters of film, spilling it on the floor in front of her. "There's your story, Mrs. Armour. We will go to the Pump Room at the Ambassador for a more pleasant evening."

At Christmas of that first year I took my first out-of-country journey, a look at resorting in the Caribbean. With photographer Philip Stern I went first to St. Thomas to a splendid little hotel called Higgins Gate. Nan and Mike Higgins, the proprietors, asked us on a Christmas sail, five sloops and a schooner-full to Christmas Bay off St. John's. We rafted up for swimming, snorkeling and cocktailing and a progressive feast from boat to boat, turkey and the whole menu. There were lighted Christmas trees on every masthead as we sailed back by moonlight, singing carols to the music of a steel band on one of the boats, ringing across the waters.

From there we went to Round Hill, a Montego Bay resort that was the season's new place to be, owned by Jamaican aristo John Pringle and his wife, the gorgeous model, Liz Binn. Noel Coward and the William Paleys had houses on the hill. In residence for the holidays were Claudette Colbert, Charles Laughton, the photographer Richard Avedon with his wife Evelyn. They all seemed to be wearing madras, the colorful Indian-made cotton plaid fabric. We photographed the charming Miss Colbert sunning on the beach in a madras two piece swim suit— "Only my left profile, please," she said. And also a rotund Charles Laughton, standing in the gentle surf, wearing a madras shirt over his trunks. Our next stop was Nassau, where the shops were full of madras jackets and shorts. Back in New York after New Year's I went to Brooks Brothers to tell them that the magazine was going to feature madras in a February issue. They ordered a window full of madras sports jackets and blow-ups of our pages in their Madison Avenue store. We had started a trend, or brought an old one back to life.

A GRAND TOUR

My next assignment was to Europe in March, 1955. It was the first of about 40 trips to Europe I would make in 15 years at the magazine, and never fear, I won't recount them all. But that first one was so special that I remember, with the help of a copy of my expense account, almost every day of it.

I flew to Paris on a Pan Am Stratocruiser, Boeing's commercial version of my faithful old Air Force B-29 bomber. Time-Life's in-house travel department booked everything for what was to be a five-week journey. There were two decks, upper and tourist and 28 sleeping compartments in first class that let down after a two hour dinner of caviar and champagne, tournedos and cognac. I was embarrassed when the time came to climb up to bed for it seemed so luxe and privileged. This was five years before the transatlantic jet put prop planes out of business, cutting flight time from 14 hours to about seven.

I had a weekend in a sunny Paris, its splendid buildings looking like Piranesi engravings, the ancient stones blackened from decades of soot and neglect in the aftermath of World War II. I was put up at the Hotel Continental on the Rue Royale and checked in with the Time-Life bureau in its nearby office in the Ministre de la Marine overlooking the Place de la Concorde. The receptionist suggested that the company would change dollar traveler checks for francs and I gave her $100 worth. When I returned that afternoon I was handed a satchel full of black market francs, with such an advantageous exchange that it was like Monopoly money.

Sterling Lord, a fellow editor at True and later a distinguished New York literary agent, was engaged to marry the daughter of a Parisian sculptor, and he had suggested that I call her family. On my second night in the city, I was invited to a cocktail party at an elegant apartment on the Boulevard St. Germaine and taken in as if I were family. I was asked to join a group of eight for dinner afterwards at a bistro on the Ile de la Cite. At the end of dinner, Rene Gruau, a celebrated illustrator for magazines and ads for Dior, proposed that as a first time visitor, I should be treated to the specialite of the house. An after-dinner liqueur came, wrapped in a napkin, poured only for me. It was clear as water and strong as sin. All applauded as I downed the glass and applauded again as the waiter unwrapped the bottle. To my horror, in it was a snake coiled around a twig. It was Viper—vee pere, the French said. The bistro was Le Beaujolais and in Beaujolais peasants believed, I was told, that the venom a viper spits into the marc as it drowns cures rheumatism. That was the beginning of my European gastronomic initiation.

A day later I flew to Milan to meet Jerry Cooke, my photographer and companion for the next three weeks. Jerry, Russian born, had lived in five or six countries and spoke five or six languages. He was to be, for the next 40 years, an invaluable contributor to Olympic and other international Sports Illustrated stories with his Nikons and his linguistic fluency. He kept a Chevrolet convertible in Europe and we drove to Venice and checked into the Bauer-Grunwald on the Grand Canal to confer with the Time-Life stringer, il Conte Zazzio. Zazzio had persuaded a family of silk merchants from Como to invite us to their very private caccia, or shooting estate, to the north of the lagoon of Venice.

No woman had been allowed at the caccia in its 400 years, one of the owners proudly told me. The land was on the flyway between Russia and North Africa. The tile-roofed clubhouse and its outbuildings, painted mustard yellow, were surrounded by 1,000 hectares of marsh and islets. The villa that Ernest Hemingway had stayed in while writing Across the River and Into the Trees was just down the road. The large main room of the club house was surrounded by vitrines of stuffed birds of every variety that had been taken by hunters over the centuries and a guest book contained lists of the great number bagged on every shoot.

First evening, we were offered our double-barreled Berettas and instructed in their loading and the rest of the drill for the next morning as we sat on high chairs around a raised central fireplace, while the staff grilled eel as appetizers with our glasses of vino rosso. Fortunately there was an ex-RAF pilot in the shooting party who had married into the family and he translated for me. Eel was another part of my gustatory initiation as was the delicious hearty veal stew and richly sauced fettuccine that we were served the first night.

Before dawn, a knock and a "permesso" from one of the staff roused each of us for a big strong bowl of coffee as we dressed for the first day's shoot. Then each guest was rowed in a skiff by a shooting guide, with his retrieving dog aboard, to a small islet. In the center of a mound of earth, camouflaged by reeds, was a concrete cistern and inside, a milk can with a cushion to form a stool. Inside the milk can were a loaf of bread, cheese, salami, a bottle of red wine and a flask of grappa. Once the guide had me ensconced, he hid with the dog in the skiff in a reed shelter behind me, waiting to retrieve my quarry. In the fading darkness, I looked up at my friends, the navigational stars, and reflected on the novelty of where I was on my fourth day in Europe--in a duck blind, north of Venice. As the sun peeped over the horizon, a horn sounded for the hunt to begin, now that ducks would be rising. Soon they appeared in honking waves, and guns were heard all around.

At about 9, the shooting was over. There were at least 50 kills. At the edge of the lagoon, men in rowboats were waiting to buy the game and great buckets of eel, trapped on the estate, for the markets of Venice. I had sat on my milk can to conceal myself and had tried to track, to lead the swift flight, but I wasn't able to down a single duck. But I was there to write, not shoot, and this was a novel and colorful story for the magazine.

Then in those first days of April, Jerry and I drove south. There was no Autostrada back then, so we were on two-lane roads that wound through every town and village and all the greening and flowering of an Italian spring. We stopped overnight in Florence and went to the San Marco to see the Fra Angelico frescos and to the Academia to see Michelangelo's David and the Uffizi to see the Botticellis. We had dinner at the Grand Hotel, and I was riveted by the skill of a lone gentlewoman across from us in black and pearls, perhaps 80. She was peeling an orange impaled on a fork. Round and round it went, not a nip in the coiling peel, not a bit of the pulp left on the fruit, not a drop of juice spilled. "It takes generations of breeding to be able to do that," Jerry said.

In Rome we stopped at the Excelsior on the Via Veneto, a block from the Time-Life Bureau. I filed my duck-shoot story and we confirmed our plans for the next stop—Positano. It was April 5, my 30th birthday, and the bureau's dashing Vatican correspondent, Principe Guillermo Ruspigliosi, organized an evening to celebrate. A group of us piled into cars and followed Bill the Papal prince in his red Alfa down the Appian Way. He had reserved at a trattoria called Il Maccellaio, or Butchery, near Rome's slaughter house for what he claimed served the best meat in Rome.

"I'll order," he said, and after our pasta course came plates of meat in a delicious brown sauce. "Shall we try it another way?" he asked. And we were served grilled meat, tender and just as delectable. "What is it?" we asked, now that we had had two servings. "It is the stomach of a new-born calf, cooked in the milk from its first suckle," he told us, "and this is the only place in Rome that serves it. Shades of Trimalchio and the Satyricon! Gastronomic initiation Number Three!

Positano, on the precipitously curving Amalfi Drive south of Naples was in its Easter festiveness, filled with vacationers for the long holiday. We were at the Sirenuse Hotel, formerly a family villa, a hundred steps up from the beach. Capri was on the horizon, 20 kilometers away. Our mission was to do a beach-fashion story and I combed the shops and found local boys and girls at the Buca di Bacca down by the rocky shore to model. It was easy to find good looking kids and stylish beach clothes, striped silk shirts, pleated skirts made of straw cloth, well tailored slacks and super knitwear, early examples of the kind of élan that has made Armani and Gucci and Missoni fashion icons.

Our next story was to be the Feria in Seville, so we drove to Naples and with Jerry's car aboard sailed the Mediterranean overnight, on the to-be ill-fated Andrea Doria to Gibraltar. Italy was left behind, but I had seen almost its full length and would return at every chance I got. As Byron wrote, "Open my heart and you shall see graven inside of it--Italy."

Seville was in full festival, a city-wide carnival that ends the somberness of Holy Week with a week long display that puts Mardi Gras in the shade. From noon until dusk, there was the Paseo de Caballos, the town's citizens on horseback in 18th century attire, the men in tight jackets and rakishly tilted hats, the women in flamenco flounces either riding postillion or in carriages. We photographed the Duchess of Alba, the direct descendent of the famous nude duchess painted by Goya. This duchess, on her beautiful white horse. was exquisitely turned out in the Andalusian traje corto, or short tailored riding jacket, with a sombrero Cordobes tilted over her right eye. We went to his finca to photograph Juan Belmondo, the legendary retired bullfighter, draped in his muletta, the matador's cape. At the Plaza de Toros, we covered the bull fights with the great Luis Miguel Dominguin. His mano a mano several years later with Antonio Ordonez would become the subject of the Hemingway report for Life which became the book The Dangerous Summer. The city was fragrant with the perfume of orange blossoms and jasmine, and the locals and visitors partied, drinking Amantillado, and dancing the Sevilliana and the flamenco until sunrise in the casitas on the elaborately decorated fairgrounds.

I parted company with Jerry at the end of the Feria story and flew to Paris for a five-day holiday. I had to change planes in Madrid and with a four-hour layover taxied to the Prado to see the Goyas and the Murillos and the master works of Velazquez. After all, this was to be my version of The Grand Tour, taken by gents of the 18th and 19th centuries. In Paris, I continued my Grand Tour survey with mornings at the Louvre, the Jeux de Paume, and the Orangerie, afternoons walking through the Marais or watching the scene at the Flore or the Deux Magots. Time-Life associates took me to a lunch given by Herve Milles, who with his brother Gerard, had a luxurious 18th century house on the rue de Varenne. Herve was the editor of Paris Match. Among the guests at the long and glittering table were

Margot Fonteyn, the great ballerina, and Suzy Parker, the model and movie star.

Herve was to become a great friend, enormously helpful whenever I needed anything in Paris. He made it possible for me, years later, to get a difficult-to-obtain private Sports Illustrated telex for the 1968 Grenoble Olympics. And he also opened doors in Paris. Once when I was visiting, he asked if I were free that evening. I was, and he picked me up at the Hotel Pont Royale in his chauffeured Jaguar and we drove to the rue Cambon. We were at the atelier of Coco Chanel. Up that famous curving mirrored stairway we arrived at Mlle Chanel's apartment. She was occupied, pinning a ruby brooch on a red lace Chanel suit worn by her favorite model, Marie-Helene Arnaud, before sending her off to the Opera. We had Champagne in that much photographed salon, with its Coromandel screens, deep tobacco suede couches, a marble Greek torso and ancient Japanese bronze deer on the fireplace. Herve's brother Gerard was her decorator. We were served a delicious dinner—I remember the Dover sole and the lovely white Burgundy especially. Chanel was wearing a hat—you have seen the picture of that look—with a large incrustation of jewels attached on one side of the brim. I only remember one bit of conversation: "And what do you zink of your President Eisenhower?" That pretty well dates the evening.

Afterwards we walked her down the Cambon to the Ritz. That is where she always slept.

I was off to London to reconnoiter once again with photographer Phillip Stern. This time our goal was to document the look and the origin of Harris Tweed. With the research done for us in advance by the London Time-Life bureau, we took the train to Inverness and puddle-jumped to the Western Hebrides. The bureau had found a crofter woman living in a stone cottage on the island of North Uist who still made tweed as it had been made for hundreds of years. When the small twin-engine plane landed at North Uist's neighbor island of Lewis, the tide was in, covering the landing strip. A boat met the plane, and the boatman, wearing rubber boots, carried me on his back and then Phillip in knee-deep water to his craft. We boated over to North Uist where the only inn had two wings, one the local insane asylum. Island inbreeding, together with the bleakness of the almost treeless bare landscapes of rock, gorse and stormy seas probably made the asylum necessary.

I cannot recall the name of the crofter weaver, but I remember her distinctly. She not only bred and raised her own sheep, but she sheared, carded and spun the wool and wove it into tweed on a primitive loom in her cottage. During the warmth of May, she sat in a chair on the rocky strand, drinking cups of tea and peeing in a large iron kettle.

90

After she dyed the wool with local herbs, seaweed or heather, she set the color with her urine.

At the Hebrides capital of Stornaway, on the island of Lewis, we photographed men wearing jackets made of the rugged material, and at the factory captured the commercial weaving of the handsome rustic water-shedding fabric, popular for its subtle Hebridean colors. Harris Tweed is as carefully licensed and controlled as Champagne, and even today is supplied to such makers as Polo and Brooks Brothers.

That was the end of my first European journey and I returned to New York having produced four stories for the magazine. My expense report of the trip seems to me today an astonishing document. I had flown first class, stayed in the best hotels—except at North Uist—entertained others and eaten in fine restaurants for five weeks and I had spent $2100. However, before I get carried away, a search of the relative value of the dollar in 1955 would indicate that I spent $17,000 in 2009 money or in five weeks about $475 a day. Relativity counts.

.

For the rest of the '50s, the magazine grew. Starting with a print order of 450,000 a week, it ratcheted up to about 600,000 by the end of the decade, a curious and complicated decade for America and for Sports Illustrated. There had been McCarthyism and the Korean War and a slow down in the GNP. The average household income was $4,650, the average house cost $30,000, and gas cost 24 cents a gallon. We were for a while a little concerned as TV coverage of sports improved, for we thought that it might compete with us. Instead, TV proved to be a windfall as the exploits and performances on the weekend of newly introduced figures, the Arnold Palmers and the Y.A. Tittles of the world, increased the public's appetite to know more when the magazine appeared on newsstands and in mailboxes on the following Thursday.

I had been made an associate editor and sent on more trips, both around the country and abroad. We produced Sporting Look stories on crew sweaters with the Penn crew on the Schuylkill, riding gear in Virginia hunt country, waterproof Loden cloth in Munich, boiled-wool ski jackets in Kitzbuhl, dapper Brits at the Epsom Derby, Scandinavian knits in Copenhagen and we profiled many American sportswear designers. Leather-and-tweed designer Bonnie Cashin became a good friend and. I frequently went with her to opening nights, to The King and I, and West Side Story, for example. At one of Bonnie's evenings, I was particularly delighted to sit at the feet of and be regaled by Gypsy Rose Lee.

Gypsy Rose Lee enchanting me at Bonnie Cashin's apartment

No matter how hard they tried, the sales department was having a difficult time selling women's fashion ads. DuPont, with its new developments of textiles for easy care sportswear made of Orlon and Dacron was, however, advertising menswear with us heavily. My responsibilities were spreading as I produced and wrote multi-page stories on amateur sports photography, the swimming pool boom, sports flying and a feature on scuba diving, how to and where to, the whole length of the Caribbean.

I had become a particular friend of Ruth Lynam, a reporter for Life in the London bureau, who helped me on many stories. We met one early September in Rome to begin a three week vacation in Sicily and Tuscany. After a week at a beach-side locanda in Taormina, we rented a tiny Fiat and drove all around that magnificent island--to Siracusa, Nota and Agrigento where our hotel overlooked the incredible valley with its stately parade of tawny Greek temples.

On location with models wearing Italian knitwear on the ancient mosaics of Rome's Appian Antica.

Then we sailed overnight from Palermo to Naples and on to the Berchielli on the Arno in Florence. "Let's go see the Pieros," Ruth said one day. I had never heard of Piero della

Francesco, but was so overwhelmed by that early Renaissance master's frescos in the church of St. Francisco in Arrezo that I vowed to come back, to travel the Piero Trail and see everything he ever painted. Forty-five years later, I did just that.

Toni Frissell had sent us photographs of elegant young women wearing brightly colored ski pants, sleekly fitting and custom tailored by Kaltenbruner of Klosters. This would not appear to be a Stop Press idea, but ski pants were black and everyone knew it. They always had been. And so were ski boots. I had come to know the principals at White Stag, a skiwear manufacturer in my True days, and I called Harold Hirsch, the president at his office in Portland, Oregon. "Will you make colored ski pants if we do a story on them," I asked." He said, "But of course." So I, with photographer Christa Zinner, went to Portland that spring of 1958. White Stag made pants of red and blue and beige gabardine which we took with models up Mount Hood where the U.S. ski team was in training. With Toni's pictures from Klosters and the ones we took on Mt. Hood, we showed that colored ski pants that had started in the Alps were crossing the Atlantic.

A Mt. Hood Sno-Cat had transported us, but at one point when I needed to go from here to there in the soft spring snow, one of the ski team girls, Linda Meyers, said, "Climb on the back of my skis and I will take you." She did and I was hooked. Next time I would be on my own two skis, not someone else's, and I went to the opening of a new resort, Sugarbush, Vermont, the following Christmas to learn to ski. It changed my life!

1960, A GLORIOUS YEAR

The 1960 Winter Olympics were scheduled in Squaw Valley, California. Jo Zill and I had, with Christa Zinner, produced, as part of an Olympic Preview, a ski fashion story there and I had been charged to find a rental house to accommodate a 10-man team of writers and photographers for the games. With weekends in Vermont, a week in Aspen, I had become an intermediate skier and was on the SI reporting team.

I will never forget the opening ceremony of those games. This was to be the last intimate Olympics. Every venue, except for the Nordic cross-country events, was in easy walking distance in the village. Parking was on a large space, a marsh in summer, that locals predicted could become an automobile graveyard if one of the great Sierra storms hit the area. It was only a few miles from the scene of the Donner Party disaster in 1848. The weather cooperated until the day before the opening when a fiendish storm dropped a foot of snow overnight. If you weren't already in the valley, you had a struggle to be there. The downhill races, always scheduled early in the 10-days of an Olympics because of the difficulty in preparing the course after heavy snows, were postponed.

Seats for the opening were inside an enormous ice arena, with huge sliding doors, like those of an aircraft hanger. They slid open to a view of the mountains beyond. The indoor arena was for figure skating and hockey. Outside was the Olympic torch site and speed skating oval, with a backdrop of the slalom hill. The snow became so heavy that you could scarcely see the teams parading into the center of the skating oval. Then the snow stopped, rising like a giant curtain. The sky cleared and the sun shone as a slalom skier carrying the Olympic torch came down the hill, handed it to a skater who rounded the oval and passed it to a skater in the arena who skated out to light the torch. Walt Disney was in charge of the opening ceremony, but he got a little help from God.

It was, perhaps, the last great winter Olympics. The U.S. men's hockey team won the gold in a match that was the equal of "The Miracle on Ice," that famous upset of the Americans over the Russians at Lake Placid in 1980. They upset the Czech team in the final, with insider advice from the Russian coach whose team had been eliminated by the Czechs. And this was during the Cold War! Americans Carol Heiss and David Jenkins won the women's and the men's figure skating gold. American Penny Pitou won two silvers, one in the women's downhill another in the giant slalom. And all America watched it on ABC! This was the first Olympics televised live in the U.S. and it was the beginning of what became an all-American ski boom.

Mort Lund, a ski reporter at Sports Illustrated, and I skied the men's downhill the day after the race. The gold medalist, Frenchman Jean Vuarnet, did it in 2.06 minutes. It took us about 15, with a few kick turns thrown in while we stopped to admire the view.

The next stop was Rome in spring. The summer games would open there in August and Jo Zill and I, with Louise Dahl-Wolfe, the distinguished photographer for Harper's Bazaar, and married-to-each-other models Joan and Bob Taft, flew to Gibraltar to take the Italian liner Cristofero Colombo to Naples. The idea was to document an American couple and their wardrobes, as they journeyed to and attended the games.

Dear Louise, who feared she would get gastritis from rich Italian sauces, had surrounded her lighting gear with bags of Pablum to ease her diverticulitis. When the customs agent at Naples, a site notorious for rip-offs, opened Louise's camera cases, we had a problem. White Pablum powder looking suspiciously like cocaine had spilled out of bags and filled her light case. A chief inspector was called. I had been through this pier before. I slipped a $100 bill into the inspector's hand and we were suddenly passed. Louise was

99

so relieved that she took all the Pablum bags that were still sealed and handed them to the official. "For the bambinos, for the bambinos," she said. I never told her about the bribe.

Photographer Louise Dahl Wolfe, the modeling Tafts, Jo Zill, photo assistant Al Linn and I camp it up at Rome's Foro Italica.

We photographed all over beautiful old Rome and at the Foro Italico, Mussolini's marble stadium, where the opening ceremony would take place. La Dolce Vita, the epic Fellini film, had its world premier while we were there. We were staying at the Hotel Flora on the Via Veneto, and the Veneto was filled with exotic characters that had been in the film, parading past the Café de Paris and Doney's. A Roman friend, the painter John Lentine, took me to a party where half the cast appeared, including Anita Ekberg and Anouk Aimee. Rome that week was La Dolce Vita, the sweet life, an extension of the film itself.

On April 1, after the Rome shooting, I took the train to Zermatt. Didi Ladd, a New York socialite and model, had a chalet there and had invited me for a week of spring skiing. Her husband, Jean-Claude Abreu, was a partner in the Zermatt ski lift company. One very special day we formed a group: Didi and her private guide, Toni Frissell and husband Mac Bacon and their guide, Louise Hitchcock and her guide and Barbara Mullen and her Swiss fiancé and ski instructor who had come over from Klosters. We were a party of ten. Through Jean-Claude we had booked a Sno-Cat to tow us on skis up to the crest of the Monte Rosa—the big Kleine Matterhorn cable car had not yet been built. Our goal: spring snow that would be forming in the April sun on the Italian side.

At the top, we waited until the sun had done its work, transforming the overnight crust into what Europeans call gross sel, big salt, and the Americans call corn snow, ball-bearing-like pellets. At about 10 we were off in a merry parade in the most deliciously forgiving snow I had ever made turns in. I was the tyro of the group with only a year of skiing behind me, but in that snow I was skiing like an expert. With the spring snow sounding like Rice Crispies beneath our skis we swooped in balletic curves all the way down to Cervinia, the resort on the Italian side of the Matterhorn. The name of the village comes from the Italian word, cervo, for deer. The Matterhorn on that south face is called Cervino, as it resembles the profile of a stag at rest.

We unanimously decided to repeat the run the next morning, for spring snow becomes mashed potatoes in a couple of hours. Without passports or tooth brushes, we checked into a local hotel. Mac Bacon had traveler's checks to take care of the bill until we could repay him back in Zermatt. And the next morning we took the telecabin up the Italian side and danced down to Cervinia once again before heading back to Zermatt. In a lifetime of skiing I have rarely had a greater thrill than those two runs, shared with that delightful group.

When the staff came back from lunch one day that summer in New York, there was a memo on all of our desks. Sports

Illustrated had a new managing editor, Andre LaGuerre. Sid James was the new publisher. We all knew Andre slightly. He had been in the bureaus in Paris and London and had run the magazine for a month while Sid James was on vacation. He was half French, half Scots. He had been DeGaulle's World War II press chief and once when Mr. Luce asked him who he saw when he went back to Paris, responded, "DeGaulle et Malraux, c'est tout."

Not only a journalist but an avid sportsman, he had covered the 1956 Melbourne Olympics for the magazine. Russia had just marched into Budapest to brutally quell with armored tanks anti-Communist risings. The Hungarian water polo team asked LaGuerre to help them jump ship and seek asylum in the United States. Andre escorted them to New York, and the magazine made political and p.r. capital of this.

One of Andre's first moves was to call me and Jo Zill to his office. The Dahl-Wolfe Rome story had been laid out for 10 color pages. "I regret that we can only run this for six pages," he said, and asked for a redesign. Was this the writing on the wall for the new regime? Jo and I wondered. Was this the end of our lovely sinecure?

In retrospect, now that I have been a top editor myself, I understand his move. The magazine was losing money, and some were afraid that Luce might kill it. Color pages were at a premium in those days, not run of the book as they became later. This was summer, high sports season, and LaGuerre was going to make this the best sports magazine in the world.

I was put at ease when Andre approved a trip to Portillo, Chile, that July, a place where our summer was its winter and where ski clothes and equipment manufacturers went to test the next season's gear. This time our photographer was Gordon Parks, the dashing and talented black member of Life's photo team. The remote mustard-colored Hotel Portillo floated alone, like the SS Normandie in a sea of Andean snow. The only way to get there was by a train that crossed the Andes on the way to or from Argentina. We had booked the Italian model Luisa Ghirladinghi to join us as she not only skied but was to be traveling in Latin America with her boy friend, an Italian artist named Oreste. My image of her arrival at the hotel, where the train stopped, is of Luisa in a mink coat sitting in a freight car on a side of frozen beef.

At Portillo, a multi-course lunch was served at 12:30 in the grand dining room, and all lifts stopped until three. I arranged for the hotel to send a picnic to the top of one of the two chair lifts for our crew so that we wouldn't waste the day. Oreste didn't ski, but rode the lift down after lunch.

One day, he departed when the chair started up again. Soon we heard a TWANG, and chairs were revolving around cables as if they were on a rubber band. Luisa, screamed and rushed to see the bottom and there was Oreste, shaking his fist at the lift. With no help from the operator at the bottom, he had jumped, throwing a chair back into the cable's wheel. The lift was shut down, and all skiing from it for the rest of our stay, and we were the least popular group in the dining room.

As long as we were that deep into South America, Jo, Parks and I, decided to make a little side trip on the way back to New York. We flew from Santiago to La Paz, Bolivia, 13,000 feet up in the Andes, and on the advice of LAN Chile, the airline, checked into a hotel for a lie down with a tank of oxygen until we acclimated. Then we boarded a little steamer to cross Lake Titicaca overnight to Puno, Peru, where I bought two bed throws made of soft vicuna fur. From there we took the day-long Alta Plano railway across the high Andean plain to Cuzco, the old Inca capital of Peru. The railway was a four-car choo choo. We were in the "buffet car," the only one with forward facing reclining seats and lunch service. The other cars had boards that ran their length, occupied by descendents of Incas in Fedoras and ponchos.

Parks almost strangled himself with his camera straps as he excitedly snapped away, first horizontal and then vertical images. Indians with llamas met us at every whistle stop, selling soup, colorful knit caps and other souvenirs. After a night in Cuzco, we took the one-car train that in those days went to the base of the monumental Inca ruins of Macchu Pichu. You could get away with such extra excursions on a Time-Life assignment in those days and in fact you were encouraged to. The company never knew when you would stumble on something that would enhance its pages.

A HAPPY CREW

Instead of being threatened by our new chief, Andre Laguerre, we flourished and our department grew and became more diverse. I was now a senior editor and we added Paul Stewart to cover men's sportswear and Jule Campbell from Glamour as women's fashion reporter. Lee Eitingon, a Life picture editor, was about to be married to Life Editor Ed Thompson and could no longer work on his staff, so she was assigned by Laguerre to us, a wise and marvelous addition. Felicia Lee, daughter of a former head of the Bank of China, became my assistant. With Felicia aboard, our happy crew began a new staff tradition, a festive Chinese New Year's lunch, inviting those people we had particularly enjoyed working with over the year. Felicia's father would suggest the restaurant and plan the many-course meal. We went, a dozen around a big round table, to a different restaurant each year, from Mott Street in Chinatown to 121st up by Columbia.

Still hoping to capture the female reader, Luce had put together a panel of women consultants led by Laura Z. Hobson, the Fortune writer and author of Gentleman's Agreement. They advised that we add Bridge as a feature, and Charles Goren was signed on to write a weekly column edited by Ray Cave who would one day become Time's managing editor.

With Jule Campbell at Bill Blass's first men's wear collection. We, being a weekly, were the first to publish it.

They also suggested that we do a weekly sport and food feature, and British-born Pamela Knight joined our group to edit it while Louise Dahl-Wolfe did the photography.

We covered vacation house architecture and new resorts. We were at Vail's opening in December, 1962, with photographer Fred Lyon. I produced a 10-page feature called Ten Square Miles of Powder. I put Liz Smith, today the country's most famous gossip columnist, under contract to write stories on Kentucky Derby and Maryland Hunt parties and to go with me and photographer Ernst Haas to Spain to document the luxurious new golf resort of Sotogrande on the Costa del Sol. Andre had added to my responsibilities by naming me travel editor.

It is no surprise that we were not exactly loved by all the other staffers. Our schedule was different from that of the rest of them. Sport's big news occurred on weekends, and the magazine was finalized on Sunday nights and went to press on Mondays. This meant that Tuesday and Wednesday were the edit weekend. Except for us. Without fast-closing stories, we worked a normal Monday-Friday week. A bigger beef was that we were using a lot of the magazine's color that many felt should have been devoted to the week's sports news. But the stories we produced had a batting average superior to most—90 percent of our stories made the magazine. In the decade from 1954 to 1964, we produced 1,000 editorial pages

I am forever proud of one story I created, with Felicia Lee as researcher. Feeling that the gear and artifacts that sportsmen used were of superior esthetic quality, we spent almost two years surveying top-of-the-line sporting equipment from around the world. We examined, by catalog and photographs, 10,000 objects, from fishing reels to jai-lai cestas, javelins and harness-racing surreys, gliders and Formula One racing cars, target pistols and baseballs, crossbows and skis. After we had narrowed our selection to about 400 examples, we asked Arthur Drexler, curator of the exalted department of architecture and design at the Museum of Modern Art, if the museum would be our arbiter of design. We of the magazine would vouch for the performance excellence of the objects. It took only two hours of showing him what we had come up with to have him say yes, and then we started the winnowing process. Half way through, Mr. Drexler said that he would like to turn this into an exhibit at the museum.

Together, we narrowed the number of selections to 110 and had them sent, from around the world, to a studio we had rented that was normally used for photographing automobile ads. Mark Kauffman of Life spent two weeks photographing the objects, big and small, with images of extreme, sculptural beauty. The SI promotion department persuaded an association of sporting goods manufacturers to help underwrite the cost of designing and erecting a parabolic tent in MOMA's sculpture garden. A Schweitzer glider was suspended in its rafters and beside the garden's reflecting pond there was a large round contemplative-viewing fishing boat made by Yamaha of Japan. At the museum's request, we had all logos removed from any object exhibited, so Head made a pair of its famous black metal skis, Spaulding a baseball and Wilson a catcher's mitt--all without brand names.

The 20-page article called Design for Sport was published in the May 14 issue of 1962. I wrote the text to accompany Mark Kaufmann's great color photographs and it was reprinted and bound as the museum's catalog for the summer-long exhibition. The objects were credited to their makers in a list at the end. We were interviewed and the show was reviewed in the NY Times and the Herald Tribune. The New Yorker published a Talk of the Town piece about me. And among many other kudos, I received from Walter Hoving, chairman of Tiffany, a letter congratulating me on "The best essay on practical aesthetics he had ever encountered." Eureka!

With television growing up and learning how to cover sport, the Olympics were even more on America's radar. ABC's Wide World of Sport had taken the name of that Saturday feature from Luce's original prospectus for the magazine. I developed pre-Olympic features designed to pave the way to the games. The season before Innsbruck's 1964 winter games I spent a month in Austria with a team of writers and photographers skiing and scouting the resorts of the Arlberg. And that spring Jerry Cooke and I were in Tokyo and all over Japan, surveying the land of the 1964 Tokyo Summer Games.

From the Innsbruck Winter Olympics I went directly to France to begin the scouting for the next site: Grenoble. Andre had named me ski editor, and so wearing all of my hats, ski, travel, fashion, resort design, architecture, I was planning an Olympic-sized preview of French skiing. My first stop was Courchevel, a new purpose-built resort high on a shoulder of the Savoie. Before Courchevel, European ski resorts rose from ancient villages at the base of mountains, shut in and dark in the winter. Courchevel's lifts and clean-lined modern hotels and chalets were built up above the valley in the sun.

After two days of touring Courchevel's magnificent terrain with Gilles de la Roche, the resort's director, I told him that I would have to leave the next day to scout Val d'Isere. Gilles said, "Well if you must see Val, meet me at the Altiport tomorrow morning." Courchevel had on-mountain plane service, a packed piste that slanted down the hill. Planes took off downhill and landed coming back up for efficiency. There was a chalet containing a restaurant and the office of Air Alpes. I was introduced to our pilot, Michel Ziegler, and with Gilles boarded a Pilotus Twin-Otter, a Canadian made STOL, or short-take-off-and-landing craft on skis, with a single, turboprop engine. It could seat eight and with its high wing and long pointed nose, looked like a duck in flight. We took off and in 20 minutes were circling above another major ski area with lifts going up every side of a valley. "There is Val d'Isere," Gilles said. "Now you've seen it!" And we flew back to Courchevel.

Instead of being disappointed, I was enthralled. On the ceiling above the Air Alpes check-in counter was a three-dimensional map of the enormous sea of mountains that surrounded us. There were red pins in places where Michel Ziegler had landed. Air Alpes was certified to take skiers, escorted by high-mountain guides, to land on plateaus on the top of a dozen glaciers. I had lunch that day with Michel Ziegler and before we had finished knew that I would be back before the season ended. Here was a unique story, combining adventure, travel, and skiing.

Michel's father was Henri Ziegler, who had been head of the Free French Air Force during World War II and later chief of Air France. As the director of Sud-Aviation he was also the man who built the Concorde. Michel had been a pilot in the French Air Force during the Algerian war and was a certified, Chamonix-trained Guide de la Haute Montagne, which meant that he could take you climbing up Mt. Blanc or anywhere else in the French Alps. He had learned how to land on glaciers from the famous Swiss pilot Hermann Geiger, who had pioneered mountain rescue flights. Michel and his lovely wife Martine became life-long friends.

I returned in the middle of March and spent two weeks in Courchevel. Air Alpes had recommended Yves Blatge, a strong and experienced English-speaking climbing guide and ski moniteur, to accompany me on my glacier story.

Haute Montagne guide Yves Blatge on the Ruitor glacier.

He was a graduate engineer and a member of the Hermes family. We went each day to the Altiport. Sometimes we took off with Michel Ziegler to check landing places, but day after day, winds on high prohibited safe glacier landings. Instead, Yves led me on day-long tours across the incredible Trois Vallee--Courchevel to Meribel to Val Thorens--over and back, while we waited to fly. Back then, with a pause for a late mountain lunch in Meribel, it would take six hours on skis to make that three-valley tour and you had to go with a guide. Today the Trois Vallee is a promenade across the largest ski complex in the world, with more than 200 lifts connecting the valleys, and more than 400 miles of designated trails. Today a competent skier can make the allez-retour before lunch.

In early April, frustrated by not flying to a glacier, Yves and I with Rob Miller, a ski patrolman from Salt Lake City who had been hanging out around the Altiport, hoping, as we were, for a glacier landing, drove over to Chamonix to ski the Vallee Blanche, a lift-served glacier that had been a must-ski destination for European skiers for 50 years. We took the vertiginous Aiguille du Midi cable car up Mont Blanc to discover that the sun was suddenly obscured by a cloud and snow. Skis on shoulders, we left the lift to walk, side-stepping, down a narrow arête with a roped railing, to the beginning of the ski terrain. Then, skis on, we started

115

our descent. After perhaps two dozen turns, Yves spied a group on a knoll far above us. Crossed skis, signal of an accident, were in the snow. "They are way off piste and shouldn't be there," he said, and then yelled, "Il y a un accident?"

When there was no reply, he said, "We have to go up there. Fred, stay here exactly where you are. Rob and I can climb faster." And they left me. More clouds came in and swirling snow. I was alone on Mont Blanc and could hardly see my feet. High above I could just make out the little gondola cars that went from the Aiguille du Midi over to the Heilbronner peak. I waited an interminable half hour until suddenly Yves came out of the mist, leading a cortege. He and others were pulling a sled made of joined skis carrying a tarpaulin-wrapped body. This was a family, two brothers and a sister, and on the sled Francoise Rubino, their 16-year-old sister. They had been roped up, realizing they had skied off piste. A snow bridge over a crevasse had given way when the young girl, the last in line, skied over it. She had died in the fall and Yves had rappelled into the crevasse to find the body.

Mountain guides carry in their pack a device that joins two skis and a tarpaulin. With ski poles attached to the sled of skis, fore and after, four people guided the created sled, two front, two back. I was one at the rear as we gradually moved through the great fields of serac, blocks of ice as big as houses, the Mont Blanc area called the Mer de Glace. When we arrived at a plateau named the Salle a Manger, the dining room, we pulled up and Yves offered his wine pouch and chocolates to the sad group. A helicopter was heard, whirring up from below. Someone had seen and reported the emergency. The ski patrol took the body and the rest of us skied down the Vallee Blanche to Chamonix. The father of the young group was chief of Haute Montagne training in Chamonix. That evening Yves went to see him to tell him what had happened.

Early the next morning Yves came to my room at the Hotel du Paris and looking up at the sky above Mont Blanc, said, "Looks like we can fly. It's calm and clear up there." We called Courchevel and Michel Ziegler said he would pick us up at the Chamonix airfield. He had with him in the plane Douglas Gorsline, a distinguished American artist who lived in Burgundy. Instead of using photography for this story, SI's art director, Richard Gangel had commissioned him to illustrate our glacier expedition. He too had been waiting in Courchevel.

At last we landed on a wide flat area above the Ruitor glacier. Douglas had his easel and stool and settled down to paint the mountainscape. Mont Blanc was on one horizon, the Matterhorn on another.

The Air Alpes Pilotus landing a ski group on the Ruitor glacier

We left him there, Michel flying away and Yves and I to cross an arête at the glacier's head. A glacier is a river of ice that finds its way by carving its channel over centuries. On the sides, or if there is an obstruction, the ice splits open forming crevasses. Sometimes crevasses are hidden by new snow, but a glacier guide can read the color of the terrain like a Bahamas bone fishing guide reads water. In the center it is a smooth thoroughfare.

In the vastness on top, we found two inches of new powder on a packed base and I, carefully following Yves, made sweeping, perfect turns down, down. In about 10 minutes we came across three Italians who were climbing with skins on their skis. They had left the foot of the Ruitor at three a.m. I always wondered what they thought when they reached the top and found Douglas, with his big straw hat

118

and his gray beard, his easel and no skis, looking rather like Matisse painting a Mediterranean port.

There is nothing in skiing like the exhilaration that comes from being alone in the wildness of a 15-mile-long glacier in ideal conditions. I was torn between a desire to keep moving and a desire to stop and look back at the perfect figure eights I had made over the traces of Yve's turns. After a while at a lower elevation, the snow turned to spring corn and then at last to soft snow. At the end of it we walked, skis off, down a mountain meadow, past summer cow sheds and finally to a little group of houses, a village called Le Mirroir, for the snow-melt lake that appears at the glacier's base in the summer. At a rustic hut, we were served a bottle of pale Crepy, the white wine of the Savoie, omelets and piz en lit, a salad of dandelion greens picked as they sprouted at the snow's edge. A taxi was called to take us back to Courchevel. The story, Turboprop to a Glacier, won an award from the Society of American Travel Writers.

SWIMSUIT

The annual Sports Illustrated Swimsuit Issue has become such an iconic publication that there are many conflicting stories about its origins and beginnings. Here is the true story.

In the early 1960's it took careful planning for our department of six, producing stories on resorts, vacation home architecture, food, travel, skiing, sports equipment and sports fashions, to make the magazine's pages. We were not guaranteed space and especially covers, as were the editors and writers of must-run events, the major sports and the major players of a season, the magazine's bread and butter. As yet there was no Super Bowl and, after New Year's Bowl games, football was over and basketball didn't go on forever.

Why not grab the third week in January, discover a winter resort in the sun and put a pretty girl on the cover? In 1963 we sent Art Kane, a photographer well-known for his color, to Puerto Vallarta with Life writer Richard Houlihan from the Los Angeles bureau. That cover wouldn't raise the pulse rate of the randiest teenager, since the girl on that cover was floating in the Pacific with only her pretty head above water.

But next season, 1964, things were looking up with a model named Babette March wearing a white leather bikini in the surf at Cozumel. This was to become Volume I of the Swimsuit Franchise. I accompanied it with a guide to skin diving in the Caribbean waters called Sneakers and Snorkels.

And then came Sue Peterson in 1965. And reporter Jule Campbell. Jo Zill, women' fashion editor, was leaving to become the fashion editor at Look, and Jule came into her own. Jule went to Los Angeles to scout for models and found this 17-year-old curvaceous blonde. Jule promised Sue's mother she would take care of young Sue, and with photographer Jay Maisel flew to Cabo San Lucas at the tip of Baja California. The cover photograph of Sue walking the Baja beach in a Rudi Gernreich swimsuit, barely containing her lovely form with its cut out sides, changed everything. There was more of Sue inside the magazine and an article by Liz Smith called The Nudity Cult. Nuns banned the magazine from classrooms. Librarians took it off their shelves. And we received hundreds of letters, mostly gee whizzes and a few "How dare yous!" from over-protective mothers of teenage boys. A jackpot! It ignited the fuse and Jule supplied the fireworks.

Sue Peterson on Cabo San Lucas, the cover that started it all

Time and SI writer Jack Olsen was in Cabo to write the accompanying travel story, Paradise on a Sand Pile. Jack Olsen married Sue Peterson, and until he died of a heart attack 38 years later lived with her, as he wrote book after book of crime and mystery stories, in the woods on Bainbridge Island, Washington.

The swimsuit and resort story grew into what became the Swimsuit Issue and eventually a stand-alone special edition of the magazine itself. At first, I went scouting to the Bahamas or to Fiji, Tahiti and Boro Boro to produce the travel story and pave the way for the fashion photography team. Then Jule and photographer, hair dresser, stylist and models followed.

Often, reflecting on the high points of my career, I wonder about some of the adventures. Were they life-threatening? Two of them probably were. On a trip to Fiji I stayed at a thatched-hut resort called Castaways on a lagoon. On Lautoka, a nearby island, there was a Wednesday market that some of the guests wanted to see, and six of us hired a large Fijian and his small skiff to take us across the channel. Midway, with a clunk, the Evenrude engine tore the transom off the back of the boat and sank. We had no life preservers and there were only two inches of transom board left above the water line. Two of the tourists were elderly women. We were at least two miles from shore on either island. If the boat had sunk, we would have been shark bait. Fortunately a ferry came chugging and threw us a line and gently, gently towed us to shore.

And once, on the beautiful island of Bora Bora, I went out with Erwin Christian, a German who had the scuba concession. Bora Bora is a typical high island, formed by a volcano rising from the depths of the sea. Around it a lagoon is created by coral reefs. The inner lagoon is a snorkler's paradise, filled with tropical reef and shell fish. When the tide is out, the surrounding reef can be walked on with sneakers. The outer edge of the atoll plunges into the depths of the surrounding Pacific. There big fish feed.

We went through a bite to the outer edge of the reef and Christian dropped anchor and with scuba gear we both went into the sea. Five minutes later, an enormous grouper swam into view and Christian harpooned it. Surfacing, he told me that we had what could be a record fish and that he would have to go back to port to get another harpoon with strong enough line to boat it. Before I could think, he sped off in his boat, leaving me holding the line connected to the grouper in the ocean at the edge of the reef. With a bleeding fish nearby!

The sharks must have been sleeping something off, for when Christian returned I still had both legs and before long he had the grouper secured but had to tow it to port. It weighed 500 pounds. The whole village came to the dock to celebrate and to anticipate a splendid luau. The local newspaper took pictures, and weeks later Christian sent me a copy with a photo and caption proclaiming that a Sports Illustrated editor had speared a record fish! Not true. But good for the island's and Christian's public relations, I suppose.

After I left the magazine, Jule Campbell did the scouting first and then directed the shoots for the next 32 years. She picked the spots all over the world, from Africa to Asia, from Australia to Brazil. And yes, true to its origins, there is still a travel story to accompany every shoot. Jule picked the photographers and carefully screened models and chose those who were less bimbo than the wholesome girl next door—only with better bodies. And by using their names, on covers and in stories, she made, or enhanced, the careers of Cheryl Tiegs, Christie Brinkley, Elle MacPherson Tyra Banks, Rachel Hunter, Stephany Seymour, and many others whose names are widely recognizable.

It became so important to the magazine's bottom line that the Swimsuit Issue became Jule's full time job. She spent months working with swimsuit designers and then scouting locations. In 1960, six years after its founding, the word was that Sports Illustrated had lost about $20 million for Time-Life. The 25th anniversary issue, with Cathy Ireland on the cover, reputedly grossed $100 million in advertising, newsstand sales, an HBO video and the annual swimsuit calendar. Jule retired in 1996 and a couple of editors have followed. They don't appear to have the firm hand on the shoots that Jule exercised, guarding the image of the models, protecting the magazine from going the Playboy route. But 54 years after Sue Peterson walked the beach at Cabo San Lucas, it is still, at a premium price, the single best selling issue of a magazine at the country's newsstands every year. All of Sports Illustrated can be found on the internet. Under its web site, SI VAULT, there are five headings to click on: Articles, SI Covers, Photo Galleries, Videos, and Swimsuit. Have a look!

SKIING THE WORLD

All sorts of things conspired to improve my skiing ability as well as enhance the number of pages we produced for the magazine. The World Cup of Skiing circuit had been established by Serge Lang of the French sports newspaper Equipe with American ski team coach Bob Beattie, and I had been named the American press member on the World Cup committee. I went back to Portillo in August 1966 to cover the FIS Ski Championships considered to be the first World Cup event. Jerry Cooke was the photographer, Bob Ottum the writer and Felicia Lee our reporter. These were to be called The Secret Race as only 300 people could stay at the Hotel Portillo, high in the Andes, and there was a handful of day-trip spectators. Most ski teams were housed in barracks nearby that had been built for Chilean ski troops. I hosted a Chilean-style barbecue under a tent in the snow for all the teams after the men's downhill; and with the dollar-peso exchange, it cost $300.

After years of domination by the Austrians, the French were suddenly the hottest ski team in the world under Coach Honore Bonnet. The Goitschell sisters, Annie Famose and

Guy Perillat, were all winning racers, but no one compared with the young Jean Claude Killy who won the downhill

Portillo 1966, at the FIS World Championships
Photo, ©, 2009, Jerry Cooke Archives, Inc.

and the combined. At Portillo that August, the French won 16 gold medals, every event but the slalom, in which they came in second.

American Billy Kidd, who, by winning a slalom silver at the Innsbruck games, had become the first American male to win an Olympic skiing medal, broke his leg in downhill training the day before the Portillo downhill. He later came back to challenge Killy in so many events that their rivalry became a mano a mano on the slopes. As our editor Andre Laguerre was French, chauvinism prevailed, and we were there with stories almost weekly, following the World Cup season for every race in the U.S. and Europe.

In the American ski season of 1966 I had produced a pre-ski- season cover story called the 10 Best Ski Runs in the U.S. The mission was to show the all-American spectrum from the hairy icy trails of Vermont, the fluffy Rockies powder of high altitude Utah and Colorado, the deep snows of the Sierras and the Cascades. It took the whole season to research, from Washington State to Vermont, with skier photographs by John Zimmerman and wonderful graphic trail portraits by Don Moss.

In the 1967 winter season I spent weeks in France paving the way for the team that would produce the 1968 Grenoble Olympics Preview issue. In Val d'Isere, I stayed at La Bergerie, the stylish little chalet run by Killy's parents. Coach Bonnet mandated that all members of the French team eat an apple before every meal. It curbed the appetite and improved digestion, he believed. So Mme Killy invented a salad called La Salade de l'Equipe de France.

Here is the recipe:
Peel and pare apples and cut in thin slices. Slice a fennel bulb thinly and also heads of Belgian endive. Add sliced gruyere cheese and button mushrooms. Toss with a vinaigrette dressing. I still serve this fresh all-white salad to guests.

I met a young Parisian medical student in Val d'Isere, Michel Delarue, who was not only a superb skier but who spoke perfect English. I hired him as a translator as I toured the French Alps, from Megeve to Serre Chevalier and many a stop between. Michel Ziegler of Air Alpes flew us in and out of many of the resorts.

Then, to photograph the French Alpine sites, came the distinguished Magnum photographer, Ernst Haas, Felicia Lee and Jule Campbell with models and very with-it and colorful French ski clothes designed for us by Michele Rossier of the company V de V. The cover and the layout combined photographs of the models and the newly built resorts, from La Plagne to Avoriaz and Courchevel. In the accompanying text, called Skiing the Kaleidoscope, I wrote,

"The best kept secret in skiing is that France has Europe's best skiing." It was until then indeed a secret.

The SI pre-Olympics team at Courchevel's Altiport: I with photographer Ernst Haas, reporter Felicia Lee, editors Roy Terrell and Jule Campbell, writer Bob Ottum and Michel Delarue

In those days Americans rarely went anywhere in the Alps but Switzerland and Austria. The appreciative French Tourist Office made a promotional film based on my quote.

I was the chief of the Sports Illustrated team covering the Grenoble Winter Games in February, 1968. I found a comfortable apartment in the press village that would accommodate us, a private telex for us to use to file our reports, and set up a team of drivers to take us to the various venues and ferry our film to Geneva to ship to New York.

131

We were a dozen: writers, photographers, reporters. The photographers, John Zimmerman, Jerry Cooke and Neil Leifer, all had assistants to carry their gear and translate, Michel Delarue with Zimmerman, my glacier guide Yves Blatge with Neil Leifer

Laguerre sat me down before we took off for Grenoble to outline what he anticipated would be the stories we would publish in the two weekly Olympic issues, down to who would probably be on the covers, who would be on this and that page in layouts. Figure skater Peggy Fleming seemed to be the only American shoe-in for a gold medal. During the games, we kidnapped Peggy Fleming. Writer Bob Ottum was in charge of her and her story. She and her mother were unhappy with the Olympic Village quarters, so we moved them to a hotel. We persuaded Peggy to talk only to us and to skate, only for us, at dawn one day in the costume she would wear in the women's figure skating final. That event always takes place on the last Sunday night of a Winter Olympics, and the problem of getting film to New York via courier to Geneva was complicated. The magazine went to press on Monday nights. We shipped a back-up cover on Thursday before the finals—just in case. And it was engraved and standing by. By good fortune, Neil Leifer's photograph of Peggy Fleming on the podium with her gold medal made it in time, and on the cover.

The ever canny Laguere was right about our covers and our layouts--except for one event. U.S. men's downhill racer Moose Barrows took a spectacular heels over head spill coming off a jump, right in front of John Zimmerman's motorized Nikons, and we telexed New York to look for the results. The multi-image tumble, in which Barrows broke his pelvis, was the opening spread of that week's coverage.

Texan Dan Jenkins, later well known for his books-into-movies, Semi-Tough and Baja-Oklahoma, was the lead ski writer. He covered golf and pro football in their seasons and in winter was on the World Cup ski circuit. Jenkins was, and still is, a towering character. He made great pals with the ABC crew so that he could actually cover a downhill race in his pajamas in the TV trailers instead of getting on a cold mountain.

Jenkins lived in the same Manhattan apartment building as Robert Redford, better known at that time for his Broadway role in Barefoot in the Park than for his subsequent movie career. He was to be the star of a movie called Downhill Racer, from a script by James Salter. The story was a loosely fictionalized version of the competition between Killy and Karl Schranz, the Austrian ski champion. As it turns out, Killy and Schranz faced each other in the most controversial event at the Grenoble games, when Schranz missed a slalom gate. He claimed he had abandoned the

133

course because he saw a spectator on the course in the fog. He demanded a rerun, but the judges did not allow one.

Jenkins had obtained Sports Illustrated credentials for Redford, and we gave him a couch in our press apartment. With him was the ski film photographer Dick Barrymore, who, like John Jay and Warren Miller, made a career of showing spectacular ski films to aficionados of the sport every fall. Barrymore, with his very visible movie gear, was disguised, Groucho Marx-like, with a mustache and dark glasses as he filmed Olympic events for Olympic background in the movie, yet to be made. No one knew Redford, not then.

The following November, when Dick Barrymore's ski movie was to be shown at Hunter College, all of us from SI went to see it. But the doors at the college theater were padlocked. The French cineaste Claude Leluche, maker of the 1966 film, A Man and a Woman, had exclusive rights to Grenoble Olympics film coverage. Barrymore had shown his film in Montreal before coming to New York, and in it there were many scenes from the Grenoble Games. The sheriff waited until he came to New York to take his film away and that was that. The next season, Downhill Racer was filmed in a recreated Olympics in Kitzbuhel. It was the film that made Redford a star.

But Grenoble had made Jean Claude Killy a super star. He won all three Alpine gold medals, Downhill, Giant Slalom and Slalom, with a zip and a panache that captured the world's attention. To this was added the overall combined medal. Killy was the first Winter Olympian to win four gold medals.

That April the first American-hosted version of Interski, a tri-annual meeting of elite ski instructor teams, was held in Aspen. Teams from all over the ski world, even Japan, came to demonstrate their techniques on the groomed expanse of Tourtelotte Park up above Bonnie's restaurant. John Zimmerman and I were there, and with his motorized Nikons, he captured multi-sequence images of balletic in-line skiers mastering moguls and open slope turns. The French team demonstrated techniques that had won the medals for its Olympians, moves called Acceleration, for giant slalom speed, Godille, or tail-wagging, for the slalom, and Avalement, or swallowing, for using knees like shock absorbers in a downhill.

We made a 10-page layout with pictures of Killy as he won his races on the Grenoble courses, combined with Zimmerman's sequences of the Interski team demonstrating the how-tos. Elliott Erwitt, Felicia Lee and I went to Val d'Isere that June, Elliott to photograph a Killy cover, and Felicia and I to write the captions with Killy and ghost-write the text for Killy's by-line, a story called Skiing Is Not a Beauty Contest. Killy skied so close to the edge that he always looked as if he were about to fall. After the cover shoot on top of still snow-covered Tignes, Killy insisted that I drive his new Porsche back up to Val d'Isere. The powerful car was a gift from Paris Match for allowing it to make an exclusive poster photo of Killy with all four of his medals. He had taken race-driving lessons from Carroll Shelby in California, and seated to my right, he coaxed me to go faster-faster on the narrow switch-back mountain road. When the cover story appeared the following November, he sent me an autographed copy signed "To Fredo le Frite, J.C. Killy." Frite was argot for fast. Killy really meant, "Fred the Slow."

I didn't know it then, but that story was to be my Sports Illustrated last hurrah. I was lured away from the magazine the following spring to become editor in chief of American Home. It was the most difficult career decision I ever made, leaving SI. I had had 15 years of learning, growth, and fun. I had learned French. I had become a good skier, in fact had skied with Killy, Stein Ericksen, Billy Kidd, Jean Vuarnet and would, before I hung up my skis many years later, ski with other Olympians, Nancy Greene, Steve Podbarsky and the Mahre twins. I had traveled with the world's best photographers and I had seen the world. And as Ken Purdy said when I left True, I had had the joy, the pleasure, of working "with all the facilities."

With Jean-Claude Killy at cover shoot on top of Tignes

AMERICAN HOME

I had known Ed Downe since my days at True. Just out of Missouri Journalism School, he joined True's staff as the editor of the magazine's shopping pages, a lucrative section of many magazines back then supported by mail-order advertising. Ken Purdy assigned young Ed to me as his editor.

Ed was a quick take and soon realized that there was a lot of money to be made in the mail-order business, and within a year or two, he himself became a mail-order mogul. He established his own mail-order company and advertising agency, left True and contracted sections for it, for Argosy and many other magazines and newspaper supplements. We had become friends and shared a summer cottage in Westport, Connecticut after he married Susan Campbell whom he had met when he was at Missouri and Sue at Christian College in Columbia, Missouri.

I am the godfather of their first child, Hugh Wisner "Cubby" Downe. On Cubby's first birthday, Christmas Eve, 1955, I was invited for dinner at their apartment on 96th street. Sue and I had a glass or two, waiting for Ed. He was in the basement with a crew of the building's between-shift employees boxing Christmas mail-orders for "fur-lined pee pots." This joke of an item was a chamber pot with a liner of mouton fur that had to be wet and stretched over the pot. The result had been over whelming. Henry Ford ordered 50 as Christmas presents. Ed had suddenly become the largest customer of enameled tin chamber pots on the East Coast!

About 9 that evening, Ed appeared and we settled for dinner prepared by their nanny and housekeeper, Bridie. Shortly, there was a knock on the door and young Sean, Bridie's son, just off the boat from Ireland, appeared. He had been put to work with the basement crew. His hands were cut from sealing up boxes and red from wetting and stretching the fur over the pots. He said, "Mr. Dowwnne, I quit, I didna cum ta America ta get inta this line a work!"

There was with Ed's business success after success. Tiger skins bought from some down at the heels maharaja, 1920's era raccoon coats—"maybe you will find brass knuckles in the pocket!" As he became successful, he bought a town house on East 50st Street and much later a splendid duplex at 834 Fifth Avenue. It had been owned by Ann McDonald Ford, ex-wife of Henry Ford. It had parquet de Versailles floors, extraordinary French hardware, and when Mrs. Ford had owned it, it was furnished with a world-class collection of 18th century French furniture.

During my Sports Illustrated years, I had seen the Downes less frequently, as we were going separate ways, but we got together at least two or three times a year, at a Christmas party or at dinner at Chauveron, one of Ed's favorite restaurants. Ed had parlayed the mail-order business into the ownership of Family Weekly, a large-circulation Sunday newspaper supplement, like Parade. I wrote a few travel stories for him, using a pseudonym, Ben Matthews, a combination of my brother's name and Mother's maiden name. Time-Life employees did not moonlight!

Ed's next acquisitions were The Ladies Home Journal and American Home magazines, bought from Curtis Publishing Company, publisher of The Saturday Evening Post. He had hired John Mack Carter, a celebrated editor of women's magazines, from McCall's, to run the Journal, and then he called me. "Would I come over and remake American Home?" He was, he said, also negotiating with Curtis to buy Holiday, then the most prestigious of all travel magazines. He would make me its editor, an enormously tempting prospect.

My friend George Trescher, who had been the brilliant marketing director of Sports Illustrated, had come into my office one morning to shut the door and tell me that he, after 15 years, was leaving to become the marketing chief of the Metropolitan Museum. "And where is your next

Olympics?" he asked. "Don't you think it is time for you to move on as well?" Ed Downe sweetened the offer when I told him I was reluctant to leave Time-Life. He offered me stock options, guaranteed to make me rich, he said.

In my quandary I went to Ralph Graves, Time-Life's genial editorial director and asked his advice. He said he would research The Downe Company for me and let me know what he thought. Meanwhile, Air France asked me to join a press trip to my beloved Courchevel in gratitude for what they said I had done for French skiing. So late that March, I took a week of ski time to think about my offer. When I returned, Ralph Graves told me that there was nothing at Time-Life in the foreseeable future that would equal the editorship of a magazine with as rich a past and a circulation of 3.5 million. "I would go," he said. "It will be good for you, even if you fall on your face!"

It may have seemed strange to all in publishing that an editor from Sports Illustrated was taking over a home-service or so-called shelter magazine. Ed bought a full page in the New York Times to announce my editorship, with a page-size photograph of me and a line that said "This man had such a great background with a sports magazine that we hired him as editor of a home-service magazine." A framed copy of that ad, yellowed over the 40 years since it was published, hangs above my desk as I write this. John

Zimmerman, my SI photographer on many a venture, took the photo.

Of course it was a challenge but it was one that was larger than I expected. The long-time previous editor, Hubbard Cobb, had been fired by Ed Downe and left the day before I walked in on May 1. The art director quit when Cobb was let go. I never met either of them, but their staffs were not eager to know me. Cobb had run a loose but contented ship, with the magazine's test kitchen staff serving lunch at his desk every day for his favored editors. But subscription and ad sales had been sliding and it was losing ground against its competitor, Better Homes and Gardens, more than I knew when I joined the fray.

On top of this, my mission was to completely remake the magazine. It was to be shrunk from Life Magazine size to Time Magazine size. It was to move from 10 to 12 times a year. It was to change from rotogravure to letter-press printing, from saddle stitched to perfect binding, starting with the September issue of 1969. I had to close, meaning finish, the half-finished last Cobb issue, July, due on press in a week. There was to be no August issue. My first issue, with all of its creative and mechanical changes, would go to press in about six weeks. The things they do not tell you!

It took everything I had learned at Time-Life to meet the challenge. I believed then and still do that no matter the subject, editing and designing a magazine is first of all an exercise in communicating effectively with the reader, using the best possible photography and art work, the most direct and comfortable typography, the cogent explaining word. The subject could be archery or architecture, football or fabrics, wrestling or wallpaper, how to ski, how to cook. You have to train your staff to think as you do, however, and with the staff that I had inherited that wasn't easy. There were territorial niches—architecture and decorating, home equipment and food preparation, gardening and remodeling, lifestyle and even beauty. Editors had their bailiwicks and their number twos were—number twos.

At Laguerre's SI, not only senior editors, but those down the line who might be helping produce, were included in the Monday next- issue planning sessions. I opened the door to my office to all, and I included all the staffers but those minding the phones. I was prepared to listen to ideas and to give by-lines to anyone who wrote copy, not just the department chief. Quel horreur! The drill had been that the Select Few would go from planning session to tell the assistants what to do. And they were the only ones who could sign an article. Just before I arrived on the scene, John Mack Carter had named Virginia Habeeb, the home equipment and food editor, American Home's managing editor. Carter was overseeing the magazine's transition from his role as editor of the big sister, The Ladies Home Journal, and later President of Downe Communications. The things they don't tell you!

Mrs. Habeeb was a professional home economist who knew the market place, and she assumed that the all-important test kitchen and the food editors were her charges as well as were the makers of GE refrigerators and Hot Point stoves. She assumed that she would edit the food pages, the letter's pages and oversee all copy. But I soon discovered that Ginny Habeeb could not write herself out of a boeuf bourguignon.

Our test kitchen was far superior to that of the Journal's team next door. Our food editor, Frances Crawford, had two test assistants and a marvel of a French chef, Jacques Jaffrey. Jacques had been a sou chef at Le Caravelle and chef at the Sky Club. His wife, also French, translated pattern instructions from French for Vogue. Jacques had taken a day job so that he could be with his family at night instead of working all evening in a restaurant. He was a marvel and a welcome discovery. I decided to make a star of him, to give him a by-line in the first issue. Not long after, Mrs. Habeeb resigned.

There were other gems on the staff. Joe Taveroni, the assistant art director, was doing a yeoman's job of supervising food and decorating photography takes. I soon made him art director. Vera Hahn, the decorating editor, was an elegant grand dame, German born, autocratic, highly respected in her field. Her number two, Helene Brown had been at House Beautiful and was a super talent. Before long I found a new managing editor Betty Klarnet who had been at Look and Woman's Day. She kept me sane and on schedule and on budget.

There was also a new publisher, Jack Dunn, who had previously sold advertising for the Journal. At our first meeting, Jack, suspicious of my SI background, said, "I don't care if a man ever reads the magazine you are about to edit." What he meant was that he wanted to position American Home as a sales-combo twin for cosmetic and beauty advertising dollars with the Ladies Home Journal, as McCall's had with its fellow publication, Redbook. This made so little sense to me that I ignored him. By my lights, men made all of the big dollar decisions in remodeling or building a house, in purchasing major appliances and men were a part of the family that we were editing for. I had been instilled at Time-Life in editing for the reader, not the advertiser. If the reader liked what you were doing, the advertiser would follow.

For our first redesigned issue, I decided that we needed a theme: Today, Yesterday, Tomorrow. The magazine had an ongoing program with the American Institute of Architects, a contest to choose the best new houses of the year with a blue ribbon jury that included the now renowned architect Richard Meier. I went to Washington to AIA headquarters for the judging. Out of it came our cover story and a handsome contemporary edition of a Georgian house--and the Today of the theme. The Philadelphia museum was mounting as an exhibition a space-age design, a circular all-plastic house on stilts that could have come from Mars. John Zimmerman, with his wonderful lighting, photographed it by moonlight. That was our Tomorrow story. And then we chose Shaker design for our Yesterday, the first of many portfolios to follow that we called The American Treasury. We photographed elegantly simple Shaker furniture in museum houses in Hancock, Village, Massachusetts, and in Old Chatham, New York. I commissioned a lovely writer, Mary Evans, to document the origins of Shaker design. Our food department produced a section using Shaker recipes, and we were off and running. Jacques Jaffrey's first of a series of Cooking Lessons, photographed by Dick Jeffreys, featured red snapper stuffed with herbs.

Instead of having test kitchen meals served in my office, I often lunched in the kitchen. Our food philosophy was to feature food that any competent person could cook from ingredients available, in season, everywhere. A dish was prepared in the kitchen, over and over for tasting, for styling, and then finally for photography. Stylist Yvonne Tarr would come to see a prepared dish and scout for accessories borrowed from antique and houseware shops.

From watching him at work, I learned many a chef's skills from Jacques that I still use today. I also learned that he had been in the Maquis, the French resistance during World War II, and imprisoned by the Nazis. On cold mornings, while standing for hours in ranks with his near-starving fellow prisoners, one would say, "Cook us a meal, Jacques." And he would ask them what they dreamed that they would eat and then tell them what a menu was to be. Then he would describe out loud and in exquisite detail how each course of the phantom meal would be prepared. Kind yes, but torture!

I believed in peopling our pages, in showing families in the decorated homes we featured, something that other shelter magazines avoided. I suppose they felt that they would date the pages when later they were put together to make a magazine's decorating book. I commissioned Super Girls, a firm of young Manhattan women to help us find people and locations from coast to coast. They were a gung-ho and energetic group of socialites who had done such things as wash down Frank Sinatra's jet, and they had planned parties for all sorts of customers including the New York Yankees.

147

The head Super Girl was Danielle Steele, yes the Danielle Steele of a raft of million-copy zippy novels. She is still as handsome in those book ads today as she was back then, when she was the bride of Claude-Eric Lazard, a principal of Lazard Freres, and lived on Park Avenue.

I also believed in shooting interiors with the kind of natural light that one experienced when actually in a room. So we used many of the Time-Life photographers who knew how to create an ambient mood that was more natural than that in the glossy, overlit decorating pages of other magazines.

Of course we joined the home-furnishings industry pilgrimage to the spring High Point market. We rented a house and Vera Hahn, Helene Brown and I would tour the enormous showrooms all over that section of North Carolina. We would find great things to build rooms around but also acres of what the cognoscenti called "Borax." At the worst of these, as the principals bowed and scraped when our Mrs. Hahn had finished her tour, they would beam as she said, "Well, you've done it again!"

For the next five years, for 60 issues, I edited the magazine. We produced American Treasury portfolios in Charleston, Newport, New Orleans, Santa Fe, Savannah, New Orleans, Pennsylvania Dutch country, and they were great successes with our readers. Advertisers, perhaps, would rather have seen more manufacturer credits. But we also gave them their due with newly designed rooms, remodeling issues, Christmas in Philadelphia, and perhaps the best how-to food pages in the business. Each month we entertained advertising agencies for lunch at the nearby Brussels restaurant, serving the Cooking Lesson dish of that month with wines selected to accompany it. I would do a slide presentation of the issue, with a low-key sales pitch, telling how much our readers loved us.

I had added a feature about prefab homes, and our architectural editor, Barbara Plumb, and I went to Louisville to scout a manufactured homes exhibition. One of them particularly intrigued us, a three-bedroom, two-story vacation house made of three units, each with steel beams framing and supporting its cedar siding and designed to be shipped on trailer trucks on the nation's highways. The San Francisco company that made the prototype had decorated it with contemporary easy-care furnishings and photo murals of San Francisco scenes. We told the manufacturer that we would feature it when one was placed on a site.

The next day, the company called me at my sister Burton's house in Louisville where I was staying. "Did I know anyone in who might want the prototype?" They would rather leave it there than ship the units all the way back to San Francisco. By most fortunate happenstance, Burton and her husband Hank Harris had recently bought land on a lake across the Ohio River in Indiana and planned to have someone frame a weekend cabin that they would finish themselves. I gave Hank my press pass to get into the exhibition and check out the house after he took me to the airport to return to New York. They bought the model, its furniture and appliances for a steal at $20,000 and it was installed, ready to live in, on their beautiful lakefront lot a couple of weeks later, ready to enjoy, which they, their kids and their friends have done for 40 years.

I also bought a vacation house, a condominium in Sugarbush, Vermont, the place where I had learned to ski in its opening season, ten years before. I couldn't let a new career interfere with my love for the sport, my territory at SI. A major incentive was America's Cup sailor Buddy Bombard's Chalet Club, created to take members on charter flights to the Alps. The club had a bus to Sugarbush every Friday night in ski season. It left at 4 p.m. from Park and 54th Street, a block from my office. Boxed picnic meals were served aboard and gallon jugs of white wine. The 300-mile trip took about six hours. I had a little Audi-100 that I left at Kingsbury's garage on Route 100 just by the Sugarbush access road. The garage would have it started and warmed up before the bus arrived. On Sundays the bus departed at 5 p.m and with the Sunday New York Times in hand one had a five-hour traffic-free trip home. I would be dropped at 57th and Third and in bed by 11 p.m. after two days with house guests and friends on Sugarbush slopes.

Sugarbush in those days had been called Mascara Mountain in a story in the Saturday Evening Post because it drew a with-it Manhattan crowd of models, publicists and columnists, like Gigi Cassini "Cholly Knickerbocker." The resort had been built by Damon and Sarah Gadd who were low key and great ski companions. Damon was heir to the Dole Pineapple family. A group of guys, headed by Michael Butler, producer of "Hair," who didn't like standing in cafeteria lines, had formed Club 10. They built a cozy lunch and drinks club up by the Valley House at the base of the gondola lift and they asked me to join. Not only was the club convenient, but it was also a place where, when the gondola line got to be a half hour long, three or four members would hire a private instructor and go to the head of the lift line.

My condo was in the first such complex built in Vermont. It was called Clairiere, French for "clearing in the woods," and it was not 300 yards from the Sugarbush lifts. Richard Colgate, of the toothpaste Colgates built them, handsome structures with great stone fireplaces. Mine was a one-bedroom, two-bath unit, with a studio living room-dining-kitchen designed to be separated from the bed-bath, with separate entrances for each. One could rent all or part in the condo pool if one chose. I bought it before construction was finished and could select the design and colors of the finishes. Since it was built into a hill side, there was an unexpected space, behind a bathroom, that was not on the plans. I persuaded the builder to turn that space into a cedar-lined sauna.

With the help of Helene Brown I decorated it with Italian-modern leather sofas which converted to two beds in the living room, an all white German-made Formica faced sectional wall unit that included storage cabinets, desk, shelves, music, TV. Kitchen counters were covered in a red-orange Formica, the bathroom cabinets faced in indigo-blue Formica. We put twin beds in the bedroom, but along one wall, end-to-end chaise lounges that could sleep two more, dormitory style.

We photographed the whole for the magazine. Of course I was able to get materials and furnishings at cost through our decorating team, and it made a good-looking and timely story, demonstrating a way to use the space in a vacation dwelling as efficiently and as shipshape as a yacht. I had friends join me almost every weekend from Christmas until Easter and mastered the often icy, sometimes rocky, Sugarbush trails. Club 10 had an annual race weekend every March, with Calcutta bets on teams and spirited fun on a slalom course and a spirited awards dinner afterwards. In summer, I rented the condo to the director of the tennis center, just across the road.

Meanwhile, I had begun to chafe because of increasing space constraints on American Home. A healthy publication formula should dedicate at least 40 percent of a magazine's pages to editorial content. But Ed Downe had due bills from many of his mail-order associates and he took up far too much of our editorial space featuring products in the back of the book, such as stitchery kits that were not up to the rest of the magazine's standard. John Mack Carter's Ladies Home Journal was so important to the bottom line that he refused to let them appear in his magazine, so they landed in American Home. I wrote protesting memos about our increasingly limited space to be creative, but to no avail. Two advertisers who had been mainstays, Armstrong, the huge linoleum and tile company, and Campbell Soup, cancelled contracts.

But even though I was working for him, Ed did not let business interfere with our friendship. He asked me to join Suzy and him for a long Thanksgiving weekend at the Lyford Key Club in the Bahamas and I went with the whole Downe family to Klosters one Christmas, Ed footing the bill. I planned our excursions and taught the kids to ski. Cubby was now 16, and daughter Hilary 13. We stayed at the Chesa Grishuna, once the favorite winter hotel of Greta

Garbo, Deborah Kerr, Audrey Hepburn, the writers Irwin Shaw and James Jones. Paul and Joanne Newman and their kids were there. For New Year's Eve, Ed entertained about a dozen at a long table downstairs in the Grishuna's Kegglebahn, the bowling alley, and good champagne flowed.

Another Christmas we went to Courchevel and stayed in the four-star Carlina, slope side. My old guide, Yves Blatge, was still teaching there, and he led us, Cubby and Hilary and me, on grand excursions across les Trois Vallee. Hilary had a teenage romance with a handsome young blond Frenchman, son of the president of The Bank of France. Neither Ed nor Suzy skied, but Ed took flying lessons up at the Altiport from Michel Ziegler.

We had flown with Michel from Paris in his scheduled Bourget to Courchevel Air Alpes flight. Ed and I sat together and Sue and Hilary in the row ahead. On the flight Ed told me of having just achieved a real estate coup. He had bought that very week an eight-bedroom house with tennis court and swimming pool on four acres on Ox Pasture Road in Southampton from the widow of Woolworth Donahue, Barbara Hutton's first cousin. Sue was hearing of this for the first time, and I saw her shoulders rise beneath her mink jacket. She hadn't even had a say or a look at what would be their summer place.

154

With Sue, Cubby and Ed Downe at Courchevel

For several years, I had rented a summer house, a 19th Century Queen Anne Victorian, on Bridge Lane in Sagaponack, Long Island, and I was invited over to nearby Southampton to see Ed and Sue's new place. The decorator Dick Ridge, who joined us for lunch said, "This has got to be changed!" The house was in the taste of a circus show girl, which is what the widow Donahue had been. There was tufted candy-pink carpet, three inches deep in the master bedroom and a sauna adjoining it had marble seating. "Ouch!" Ed said, "but a little paint and a little fabric should fix it up."

He was ever the perpetual glad-handing host. Over the summers the house became a country club. He imported a chauffeur, a maid, a cook from the Lyford Key Club which was closed during the summer season. Friends of the young Downes, particularly Cubby, were there in squads, drawn by perpetual buffets of lobster salads and hamburgers on the grill. Sue, a fine tennis player, could hardly get on her own tennis court on weekends as people she never knew kept it occupied. Ed was a good player too, but he had injured a knee playing football at Hotchkiss and rarely came on the court. Instead, he had a major gin rummy game going in the air- conditioned library for most of the day. Thereby hangs a tale.

Twice the Downes invited me to join them at villas that Ed leased in Villefranche high above Nice. In June, 1974, we sailed on the France, with a group of their Missouri friends, including Charles and Carol Price. Charlie was a Kansas City banker and later Ambassador to the Court of St. James. It was the last transatlantic voyage of the beautiful ship, and caviar and Roederer Cristal Champagne were served lavishly as the crew emptied the ship's larder.

While at the Villefranche villa, Ed told me that he was putting the publishing company up for sale and that he was giving me lead notice as he had a prospective buyer and didn't know if he could protect my deferred investment with the company should it change hands. When I returned to New York, I called friends at Time-Life and in a week's time was hired as an editor at Time-Life Books. Raymond Mason, a Florida entrepreneur, bought Ed's company and continued to publish the Ladies Home Journal, but American Home, with Helene Brown as its new editor, lasted only another year. Before Mason took over, Ed, good as his word, sent me my deferred investment.

Ed and Sue Downe were divorced before long. In August, 1986, Ed married Charlotte Ford, daughter of Henry Ford II, in Southampton. As an eerie consequence, Charlotte had married the man who now owned the Fifth Avenue apartment that she and her sister Anne had shared with their mother. Ed and Charlotte asked me to dinner one night, and at a long table, I was seated between Barbara Walters and Charlotte Curtis, who was the society reporter of The New York Times.

But then Ed came a cropper. He was on the board of Bear Stearns and in 1992, he was charged by the United States attorney for insider trading and making, with some of his cronies, an illegal $23 million. They included Martin Revson of Revlon. It is assumed that Ed had talked too loosely over his gin game of IPOs, (initial public offerings,) about to happen and that one of the hangers-on around his pool had blown the whistle. Ed pleaded guilty and forfeited his large collection of contemporary art, the Fifth Avenue apartment and the house in Southampton. Charlotte Ford stayed with him, but only through the trial, after which they divorced. In the last days of the Clinton administration Ed's friend, Connecticut Senator Christopher Dodd, obtained a presidential pardon for Ed.

TIME-LIFE BOOKS

The Time-Life Books division was a phenomenon that had grown since I had been away from the company during those five years at Downe. Its big success was selling series of books to subscribers, a new volume every other month. Among the big successes were series on Cooking the World's Best Cuisines, The Old West, World War II, Gardening, Sailing, Photography. Each series was staffed like a magazine with an editor, art director and writers and researchers. Many of the senior staff had come from the recently defunct Life, that great and impactful magazine that had died in 1972. There was a whiff of this being a sort of job of last resort about the place. Last resort or port in a storm, I was glad to be there at my old company. I would gain retirement seniority to add to my 15 years at SI.

My first assignment was to edit the Photography Annual, an addition to the popular Photography Series. I submitted a plan for an annual that was miraculously approved with little question, considering that I was at that time an outsider. But I had learned a great deal about photography in my editing and quickly threw myself into the job of making the book. The toughest parts were the technical pages, examining the quality of the mechanisms of the current 35 mm Single Lens Reflex cameras, for example, which were the most used by serious amateurs. For glamour, I suggested a portfolio of the archival work of the photographer Horst, with iconic pictures of the Duchess of Windsor and Coco Chanel and Mrs. Harrison Williams. Horst in his 80s lived in Great Neck, Long Island, and I went to interview him with Gene Thornton, photo critic for the New York Times and a writer who did many of the essays in the book.

When the photo annual was finished and off to press, I was asked by Jerry Korn, the chief editor of the books division, to come to the aid of a series that was in trouble, missing deadlines right and left. It was the Sewing Series. Oh my! I suppose that my American Home background told him that I knew something about the subject. But I had no alternative, and for the next year I struggled to make a silk purse out of a sow's ear, or lead my inherited staff into doing that. As I remembered communicating in publications was a matter of good art direction, good and cogent explication of the subject, the laborious editing task began.

We had a staff of a dozen writers and researchers, a picture editor, an art director and a slew of contracted consultants including a needlework expert who tested everything from knit to crochet instructions, a tailor who made patterns and tailored slacks and jackets. a decorator who designed and gave instructions for slip covers, drapery and pillows. We would produce a book in eight weeks and there were six to go when I took over, a year's work. To my amazement, two of the books that I directed, the Photo Annual and the Sportswear Sewing edition, bound in orange corduroy, won awards from the American Institute of Book Designers.

I was more at ease with my next assignment, assisting Oliver Jennings, the director of planning for the books division. A small staff of art director, editor and a writer made elaborate color brochures filled with example layouts, covers and contents of a proposed series. These were used as mailings to prospective customers, asking them to reserve a first edition to test their interest. Startups were too risky, too costly, to be launched without tests to see if they would fly. I proposed and wrote several ideas that were tested. One was on anthropology called The World's Vanishing Peoples from pygmies in the Congo forests to Amazonian Indians and the blue men of the Sahara. Another was called How America Lived, which would examine day to day life as experienced by people from the earliest settlers through many decades, Colonial Times, Federal Times, Plantation Times, Prairie Times.

Shortly Time-Life announced that the book division was to be moved to Alexandria, Virginia, away from the high rent of Rockefeller Center. The most successful series, created in the past, while still prospering, were finished, so the move was obviously also a way to downsize. Many employees, entrenched in New York, with kids in schools and spouses with careers there as well, would not go. Jerry Korn took me to lunch and asked me to move with them. If I would go, he would make me the planning director. I told him that I would let him know in a couple of weeks. It was May, 1976, year of the American Bicentennial.

EAST/WEST NETWORK

Networking. In the maelstrom of New York careering, it is a way of keeping up with what's what and who's who. I belonged to several networking organizations: the American Society of Magazine Editors, the Society of American Travel Writers, the New York Travel Writers, the New York Athletic Club.

At a press party given by Pan Am, I met Peter Buckley who was the editor of the airline's magazine, Pan Am Clipper. He told me that East/West Network, the Los Angeles company that published it, was contemplating opening an office in New York. Since I had experience in editing and writing travel articles, this interested me and I found the owner's name in a copy of the magazine and called Jeffrey Butler to introduce myself. When Jeff came to New York the following week, we had lunch at 21.

We talked for hours about magazines. He had been, side by side with Maureen Reagan, daughter of Ronald Reagan and Jane Wyman, public relations director for PSA, Pacific Southwest Airlines, a California commuter headquartered in San Diego. He proposed that he create a magazine for them and got a go-ahead if he could make it financially feasible.

To do so, he persuaded Continental Airlines to join with them, left PSA, and began a small publishing company. Inflight publications had been little more than company produced leaflets in the seat pocket containing route maps and safety instructions. Swiftly, he added magazines for other airlines--Hughes Air West, Western Air Lines, Frontier. When he signed contracts with Pan Am, Delta and United Air Lines, the country's largest international and national carriers, he was in big-time publishing.

Jeff in his late 30s was full of charm. He wanted to know what I thought of his magazines, and after our meeting, sent copies to my apartment. I poured over them, at first to understand the method and the mission, and then to scan them, page by page. I annotated each one, and found them capable but not up to the standards of the magazines published by Time-Life, of course. Headlines were lame and captions were obvious and clunky. I had preached caption-writing to my editors: A caption should not be a label, reciting the obvious, such as "This is the Matterhorn or Lake Como, or Mr. and Mrs. Gotrocks" but titillate with an extra point about the place, the object, or the people in view. "Mr. and Mrs. Gotrocks have been sweethearts since they met as teenagers in high school."

Jeff had hired a researcher to characterize inflight readers and determined that most frequent flyers were affluent business men. The editorial matter for each publication was aimed at them, but each magazine was editorially unique. There were, of course, pages dedicated to route maps and inflight movie schedules, and for overseas flights, duty free items. But the ads, most of them, were the same for all, across the board. Hertz was on the back cover of all of them. That was the strength of the network, and the basis of the company's success. By a formula of delivering to an airline one magazine for each 10 passengers, he had a print order of more than one million copies a month. And instead of incurring the cost of mailing to subscribers, the airline provided the delivery system. The readers of them were all, for ad selling purposes, the same demographic profile passenger.

I wrote a critique of each magazine, pulling no punches; but I also included ideas for features that might be considered for the future, and shipped the package off to Jeff in California. For two weeks I had no response, and then one day a call. "I will be in New York next Monday. Are you free for dinner?" Of course I was.

Jeff had an apartment at the Essex House on Central Park South, and I met him there for a drink before dinner in the hotel's dining room. East/West had just signed a contract to publish Eastern Air Line's magazine. Eastern was headquartered in Miami and one of Eastern's demands was to have an editorial presence in New York, not in Los Angeles. East/West already had an advertising office at 488 Madison Avenue, and Jeff planned to house an editorial department there. He offered me the job of editorial director, not only of the Eastern office but of all the magazines, East and West. He would move Pan Am's and USAir's magazines back east. Peter Buckley, East/West's eastern correspondent and de facto editor of Pan Am Clipper was already ensconced there.

No, he didn't believe in giving contracts to management, but he offered me a financial package that was not only attractive, but timely. I did not want to move to Alexandria, Virginia, away from New York, Publishing Central, so after sleeping on it that night, I called him the next day to accept the position. Here was another entrepreneur, cut from the same self-made cloth as Ed Downe. And I was off to a new adventure and challenges as yet unknown.

The first surprise was the plan for the new magazine for Eastern. It was named Eastern Review and Jeff had promised that a committee of experts would review selections that editors had gleaned from current publications, books and magazines, a la Reader's Digest, and package them as a magazine for the busy traveler. The cover design was a grouping of magazine covers from articles featured. This device made the right to reprint attractive to other magazine publishers. Good idea.

Early on, I met the committee at a lunch in a private room at the Italian Pavilion. They were well known names: Polly Bergen for beauty, Dick Schapp for sport, Robert L. Greene for style, Elliott Janeway for finance, Frances Koltun for travel. The East/West staff would make the selections and send them to committee members for approval. Bad idea.

This turned out to be a real stumbling block. Even though Jeff was paying them each $500 a month, they were very lackadaisical about their responses. Since the public relations or advertising director of every airline reviewed everything that went into a magazine before publication, the committee was just one more layer one didn't need, I thought. But for a while, that is the way we did it.

Next I went to Los Angeles. The offices were on two floors of a building on Wilshire across from the Los Angeles County Museum. Los Angeles was minor league publishing territory compared to New York, and the talent pool was limited. Each magazine had a staff of editor, art director and an editorial assistant. Common to all of them was an overall art director, a managing editor and a photography team. There was even a photo studio to make covers and illustrate articles. Jeff had established sales offices nationwide, in Dallas, Miami, Chicago, Los Angeles, and New York.

I stepped into my responsibilities gingerly, feeling my way. Everyone was suspicious of this East Coaster, particularly in the West. I can't blame them. I carefully minded my Ps and Qs and tried to be a diplomat. They were a clannish group, partying together on pot and vodka-fueled weekends, having office romances that came and went. But this was Los Angeles in the 70s.

Jeff had been in business about five years and had established a network of trades, notably with rent-a-car companies and Marriott hotels. His New York flat in the Essex House was a trade with Marriott. I became an intercontinental yo-yo, traveling monthly between New York and Los Angeles as I learned the ropes and staffed up New York. There were monthly planning and financial review meetings in Los Angeles. And one by one I visited each of the airlines in their headquarters. Jeff Butler had built a $50 million a year company as its sole proprietor.

Now that I was spending a part of every month in Los Angeles, I had no time to go up to Sugarbush, so when the tennis pro who rented my Vermont condo each summer offered to buy it, I sold it to him. I tried to buy the Sagaponack house that I had rented for eight summers, but the owner wanted to keep it in the family, so I began looking for a place to buy, staying with friends in the Hamptons on weekends. I must have seen 40 houses before I found one that I liked. It was on a half acre on Roxbury Lane in Wainscott, a small hamlet in East Hampton surrounded by farms, ponds and ocean beaches, settled by the English in 1660 Generations of Osborns and Hands still own acres of it.

It was not far from the Atlantic beach, only two streets from Montauk Highway, the fish store, the liquor store, the Wainscott Post Office and the Hampton Jitney stop, which made it convenient for guests without cars. The Jitney had just begun service, pleasant big European style buses that run from midtown Manhattan, 100 miles away, through Southampton, Water Mill, Bridge Hampton and Wainscott before going farther east to East Hampton Village, Amagansett and Montauk. Today, as I write this, it transports a million or more passengers a year, running hourly from six am until 10 pm in each direction.

The Wainscott house had belonged to Florence Fabricant, food writer for The New York Times and her husband Richard. They had built it when they had two young children. I was attracted by the layout, a large central room with an island kitchen on one wall, and, on each side, two bedrooms and a bath. The ceiling of the central room was 14

169

feet high, surrounded on all four sides by clerestory windows. There was a free-standing Swedish fireplace and a large deck at the back surrounded by scrub oaks. Neither the decoration nor the landscaping was to my taste—brick-patterned linoleum covered the floors and the pine paneling in the major room had turned orange in the flooding sunlight. But I could fix all of that, and the price was right. Before I signed the deed, I asked Jeff Butler if he might move me to Los Angeles in the future, and he replied that he would move the whole company east before he did that.

Not two months later, Jeff asked me to move west to run the editorial content of the magazines from the west coast office, with the eastern office answering to me. Why? Perhaps because he had married Erin Clarke, a Pennsylvania girl who loved California, looked like a cheerleader and was a cosmetics company public relations director. I would commute in the other direction, LA to New York. I had a rent stabilized apartment that I treasured in New York that was irreplaceable and far cheaper than hotels on days I would have to be there. The company would pick up the New York rent. When I told him that I had bought the house in Wainscott, in East Hampton, after he said he would not move me west, he said, "But what a good investment!" He was right.

Once I was in Los Angeles, with the New York rent taken care of, I decided to buy there as well. I wanted to show my commitment to both my position with the company and to the city. A good friend who had worked for Life in New York, Bob Carpenter, had a two bedroom apartment in a Spanish-style compound and he took me in whenever I was there for a short stay or a week. Bob was from a socially prominent Los Angeles family and took me to lunch at the California Club and on tours of the sprawling city. I still had enough of my Time-Life savings to make a down payment, and with Jeanne Rains, also an old New York friend, now in the real estate business, began to look. We scoured the LA basin from Santa Monica to old Hollywood. Beverly Hills was too pricey, downtown too far from the office. I did not want to be a part of the endless Southern California commuting scene. I found a typical 30's style stucco and tile-roofed bungalow on Huntley Drive in West Hollywood only 10 minutes from the Wilshire office building. I bought two houses in six months!

The Huntley house needed a lot of work. I found a carpenter to knock out a wall of the master bedroom and open it, with sliding doors and a deck overlooking the garden. After all, this was sunny California! It needed painting, inside and out. There was a young Greek named Panos who worked in the garage in my New York apartment building. He had graduated in engineering from a college in Athens and was

171

striving to get ahead in America. He always had my Mustang washed and shiny when I picked it up on weekends and he had painted my apartment in New York. Impressed with his work ethic, I asked him if he would like to go to Los Angeles to paint my new house and he jumped at the chance. He and a fellow Greek went out on a Greyhouse bus—I bought the tickets. I left my California car under the port cochere for them to use. And I had bought two mattresses that were on the floor in the bedrooms.

The Los Angeles Design Center, called The Blue Whale, because its round-roofed architecture was housed in blue glass, was just around the corner. I used my American Home experience and my press pass to get access to show rooms and bought, from Stendig and Knoll, Italian sectional seating chaises for the living room, Breuer designed steel and Formica end tables, Meis van der Rohe chrome and raffia chairs and chrome tent lamps. I covered the floors in sisal and tiled the entrance hall. In Santa Monica I found English chests that had been paint-stripped to their pine. For the deck, I found a 10-foot-square Italian market umbrella and Bertoia wire chairs. It was all neat, with-it and attractive. At first I would have to make strip maps to guide me from one place to another around the sprawl of the city. Jeff furnished cars, on trade of course, to all of his top managers, and I had a deep green Cadillac Seville. After a while I felt at home in Southern California.

The Butlers had leased a house high on a Beverly Hill that had once belonged to Cole Porter. Its swimming pool terrace overlooked all Los Angeles from the Pacific to the downtown skyscrapers and the Santa Monica Mountains. They entertained frequently, and at one dinner party I met Kurt Kreuger, who played the young Nazi in many a post World War II movie. Kurt had just bought a condominium in Aspen and he asked me to come for a week of skiing. Over the years to come, I would join Kurt and a bunch of other friends on Aspen ski holidays every year until we both reached our 80s.

Maureen Reagan, a friend of Jeff since the early PSA days was now the daughter of a president. She was to be married and asked Jeff if she could have her wedding reception at his house. The prospect of having the President of the United States as a guest had the Butler's in a dither. They got new draperies, a new gardener and did the place up even more luxuriously. The Secret Service came to check the security of the neighborhood and the house. Invitations were out, catering and music booked. On the day before the reception, Jeff received a call from Maureen. Her mother, Jane Wyman, even at odds with her ex-husband Ronald Reagan, had decided to host the reception herself at the Beverly Wilshire, but thanks anyway. And to Erin and Jeff, please come. The evening after the debacle, the Butlers had a super party with all of the catered spoils of the reception. I remember two things, ice sculptures filled with caviar, and the rage of Vaneeta Butler, Jeff's mother.

The company had sales meetings annually, in such comfortable places as Palm Springs, Bermuda, Hawaii, Dromoland Castle, Ireland, Sanibel Island and Ponte Vedra, Florida. Jeff brought Gloria Swanson to Ponte Vedra to inspire us. We were doing better magazines, with expanded budgets allowing us to publish portfolios by such splendid photographers as Ernst Haas, Karsh, and Gordon Parks and to pay competitive fees to freelance writers. Inflights were no longer just quick-glance publications. I had a strong feeling that people did not appreciate something that cost them nothing, and with the competition of drink and meal services, movies and such on-board work as meeting planning and expense accounting, our challenge was to grab the seat-belted reader with covers and cover lines.

One of the stories that I produced for United led to lifetime friendships. I was fascinated by the Los Angeles gallery scene and spent many Saturdays at gallery openings on Melrose and in Santa Monica. Not far from my house was a gallery called Gemini. It produced—still does—limited edition lithography for such major artists as Jasper Johns, Robert Rauschenberg, Ellsworth Kelly, Claus Oldenburg and David Hockney. Their archives are now in the collection of the National Gallery in Washington. I spent many a Saturday afternoon at Gemini and got to know Sidney Felson, the owner, and Joni Weyl, soon to be his wife.

They gave an artist weeks at a time to work privately with their world-class printers. Fascinated, I assigned a writer and photographer to delineate their story. Sidney persuaded David Hockney to come to the gallery and make a drawing in black touche as our photographer worked. Limited edition lithography was at the height of its creativity, and collectors were seeking prints. I needed art for my Los Angeles abode and bought a David Hockney called Celia Musing. It is framed in the gold leaf that Hockney selected for the exhibition of a series of six versions of Celia, his friend Celia Birdwell, an English fabric designer. It hangs, still loved, over the mantle of my Long Island house. I later acquired from Joni Weyl's newly opened Soho edition of Gemini an Ellsworth Kelly, a seven-foot long piece from his arch series. It now hangs, in perfect juxtaposition, on a wall in Wainscott, its vibrant green curve echoed by the trees behind a soaring triangular window.

Jeff craved publicity and I persuaded Don Morrison, media editor for Time Magazine, to write about the phenomenal success of Jeff Butler's East/West Network. It called him the high-flying millionaire publisher. That was another Bad

Idea. Jeff didn't own our magazines and that was his Achilles heel. He had five-year contracts to publish them, and after that story appeared, the wolves began to circle. ABC and CBS both at that time had magazine divisions and they were interested. So was Hearst. So was Ziff-Davis. When renewal time came up, there was competition for contracts, offering larger percentages of profits to the airlines, one by one. At first, Jeff's charm and the quality of the magazines won the day, but we were not out of the woods.

In 1979, an American Airlines DC 10, losing an engine on take off, crashed at O'Hare, killing 273 passengers and crew. For a while, all DC 10s in every airline fleet were grounded--with the loss of East/West readers. And there were airline strikes troubling the friendly skies and the advertisers supporting our magazines.

One thing rankled Jeff and Erin. There was no advertising for women's products, fashion, beauty, health—Erin's field. And no editorial either. The two of them came up with an idea. Let's create a new magazine, something Jeff would own, call it All In Style, aimed at women and distribute it through Sunday sections of metropolitan newspapers, as Family Weekly and Parade were distributed. Give it to them free! I was summoned up the hill to confer day after day, particularly after the two of them had had late night sessions planning layouts and story ideas.

Beware an entrepreneur who has one brilliant idea. He may think that all ideas that follow are just as original, just as brilliant. For a while, Jeff wanted me to go back to New York and staff it up, but I had so little belief in the project that I begged off. We did produce All In Style. We hired David Bruehl from Avenue Magazine to edit it in New York and Rachel Crespin, a Harper's Bazaar fashion editor, to produce the fashion pages, but no big newspaper would take it as a free insert. Jeff had to pay advertising rates for that, and he ended losing $2 million over the year it was published.

It was 1983 and I had lived in my Huntley Drive house and worked in Los Angeles for five years. I had been hesitant to go west in the first place, but I was reluctant to leave it when Jeff and Erin decided they wanted the publishing and the social life of New York. We were all going back East, and I rented my house, furnished, to screen writer Carol Eastman. But at least I had learned how to navigate the freeways and the byways of Los Angeles and what it meant to live in sun kissed, smog-fumed Southern California.

I went back to 57th Street, and the Butlers, now with two children, Drew and Emily, lived for a while in a penthouse on top of the Essex House and began looking for a Westchester estate. They found Brookside, a spectacular place in the very heart of Rye, New York. It had been the home of a granddaughter of Henry Flagler, the Standard Oil and railroad tycoon who built Palm Beach. The large Georgian house had a suite of living and receiving rooms, a library, a formal dining room, breakfast room, hotel size kitchens and laundry on the ground floor, and up a spectacular staircase, two floors of large and comfortable bedrooms. Its gated 14 acres, filled with daffodils and rhododendron, had two swimming pools and a tennis court. Jeff had a brown Rolls Royce, the twin of the one he had driven in Los Angeles. But now he had a driver to take him to the city.

He named me editor in chief, and in a couple of years president and publisher. In truth I was president and publisher in title only, for Jeff and financial officer Mike Sultan made all of the business decisions. We often made tense calls on our airline partners when contracts were up for renegotiation. Sometimes we lost. Ziff Davis stole away Pan Am and US Air, for example, and a Miami company won Delta away from us.

No doubt this caused Jeff to look more intensely for another medium, and along came Dial, the magazine of Public Television, founded by Jay Iselin, president of New York's

Channel 13. Iselin had been an editor at Newsweek earlier in his career and created, with the network stations in agreement, a magazine to give, along with a central section filled with cultural articles and interviews with stars of the shows, program schedules tailored for each market, a la East/West and the airlines. Dial was looking for another publisher, and Jeff visualized it as an opening to produce city magazines all across Public TV land. The contract stipulated that he bring aboard the existing Dial staff, a group of perhaps 10 editors and art directors.

This turned out to be a mixed blessing. On the staff of Dial were some talented people, including David Doty, an editor. But the effort to launch Dial was another costly one, and after investing more than $2 million, it went the way of All In Style. Doty stayed on with East/West in increasingly important positions, eventually becoming editorial director. David is still a close friend and has a weekend house near by in Wainscott.

The crew at East/West had moved to three floors on East 51st Street. A splendid Chinese restaurant, Larry and Annie Lo's Tse Yang, on the ground floor and its bar became our after-work gathering place. Jeff turned Brookside into his headquarters and management meetings were held there. Brookside could accommodate all of us.

Now that I was back east, it was time to work on the Wainscott house. Harry Bates was an architect I had admired and published in both Sports Illustrated and in American Home. He had been at Skidmore, Owens and Merrill and adapted the Skidmore modernist ethic of steel and glass towers into vacation houses just as carefully crafted in wood and glass. His office was now in Sag Harbor, Long Island. Harry designed a new façade, a new entrance hall instead of a door right into the living area, closets, and above all a real and spacious kitchen.

A 57th street neighbor, Bob Schaeffer, asked me to spend a weekend at his house in East Hampton while I checked on the construction. Bob was the marketing director of The Leading Hotels of the World, and we knew each other through many travel industry events. We became close friends and went to Aspen to ski with Kurt Kreuger that April and almost every ski season for the next fifteen years.

We also teamed up to play doubles every Saturday on Sidney Butchkes's court in Sagaponack every March, Bob had to go to World Travel Market in Berlin and afterwards I would meet him for a week or two of skiing in Wengen, Gstaad, Zermatt or Courchevel. Bob has been my companion for the last 26 years.

With Bob Schaeffer in Zermatt

Jeff and Erin Butler became socially active in Manhattan. Once he took a table for 10 for the White Russian Ball. He asked me to escort the beautiful redhead actress Arlene Dahl. Her husband Marc Rosen was in Europe on business. When we reached the receiving line at the Plaza Ballroom, I overheard Jeff introduce Erin, a native of Pittsburgh, with this statement: "This is my wife Erin. She's a Frick, you know." Quell folie de grandeur! Erin was no Frick. Bob's former wife Rita was, however. She was a grandniece of Henry Clay Frick.

Henry Hale had died, and Mother, after almost 40 years of marriage to him, was living alone in the house they had built together in Tuscaloosa's Guild's Woods. Burton went for a visit and was concerned that she wasn't eating correctly. Now 85, she had lunch most days at the University Club, only two streets away, but little else during the day. We decided that the time had come to find a more secure place for her. Burton visited the Episcopal Home in Louisville, near her home, and found it just the place. The rooms were pleasant, the food good, and there was an active group of bridge players to entertain her.

In June, 1987, we all descended on Tuscaloosa to give her a farewell party at the University Club. Almost 100 family and friends came. Friends had decorated it with lavish bouquets, and the club prepared such southern canapés as Virginia ham and beaten biscuits, crab dip, and deviled eggs. It was Tuscaloosa at its very best as Mother's friends of 50 years, their kids and grandkids came to say goodbye. The next day, after Sunday at Christ Church, the family went in three cars to the Tuscaloosa Country Club for lunch. I drove Mother, and as we parked she said, "You all are certainly lucky," to which I replied, "But of course we are Mother, we have you." She replied, "I mean, I could have raised hell." That was typically Mother, stoic and realistic.

All my adult life, aware that I had no doubt inherited the Smith heart from my father and grandfather, I had had annual checkups. One late September day in 1990 as I walked home from the office carrying two brief cases, I felt a tightness in my chest and sat on a garbage can until it passed. The next morning I called my cardiologist, Bob Ascheim, who had offices on 57th Street and Sutton Place. After he examined me, he recommended that I check in the next day, a Friday, at New York Hospital for an angiogram.

At Mother's goodbye-to-Tuscaloosa party, with Burton and Ben

The result showed that I had a 90 percent blockage in my left descending anterior coronary artery. Bob Ascheim came to my bedside and said that I would probably need open-heart surgery. Later Dr. Karl Krieger, a member of the top team of cardio-thoracic surgeons of the hospital, came to tell me that I would need a triple-bypass and he was ready to operate on Monday morning. I was kept in a hospital bed all that weekend and on Monday, October 1, I was rolled into surgery.

Curiously, I had no fear. My heart had not been damaged by a heart attack and I was in good hands. I thought of my father and wished that he had had the chance I was to be given. He died too soon, but he had left me with the knowledge that I would have to look after my own heart's health all my life. The heart-lung machine that made it possible for this operation had not yet been invented in his day, nor had the diagnostic precision of an angiogram, or the wonderfully effective statin drugs. In fact, few had even heard of cholesterol until the 1960s.

Art Director Bob Cato's get-well card after my surgery

I was in the hospital 10 days—today they toss you out in four or five. Fortunately Dr. Krieger had used the pectoral artery along with sections from a vein in my leg to make my grafts. It had been determined that this lessoned risks of reblockage. And then I spent weeks recuperating and getting my strength back. Ski season was approaching and I wondered about Aspen's altitude and my replumbed heart. Aspen's base is at 9,000 feet, its summit about 11,500. I called the editor of Aspen Magazine and asked if she could use an article on skiing after heart surgery. My goal was to follow the advice of the experts as I moved back into skiing and at the same time to ease the fear others might have by showing the way. She was very interested.

Bob and I went to Aspen in January, three months after my surgery, and stayed in Kurt Kreuger's condo, a short walk from the Aspen gondola lift. I had scheduled a physical with Dr. Barry Mink who was the physician of the U.S. cross-country ski team, and interviews with an emergency room doctor who had been on two Everest climbs, and with the head of the ski patrol. Dr Mink gave me a useful and memorable motto: "The secret of a long and healthy life is to acquire a chronic disease and spend the rest of your days taking care of it."

I checked out in good health and I followed their advice. Go easy at first. Swing your legs on lifts. Drink lots of water. Check your pulse. I asked Fritz Benedict, Aspen's founding architect, a gentleman who had had two heart surgeries, to ski with me. He was in his late 70s and it was all I could do to keep up with him. After he barreled down a field of moguls, I asked him if he got breathless or had fear. "No," he said, "I just listen to my body. Life is meant to be pursued and enjoyed." The article that I wrote for Aspen Magazine, called From Bypass to High Pass, was the beginning of what became an active freelance career when I retired from East/West.

For Jeff, things were getting rocky on the business front, and as it turned out on the home front as well. Eastern went out of business and Pan Am, which we had gotten back from Ziff, soon followed. Those airlines that remained, most importantly United and Northwest, were asking for a larger share of East/West profits. If the boss could live in such splendor with a chauffeur driven Rolls, maybe he was getting too much out of their arrangement. Before long we were having cash-flow problems. Printers and paper companies were not being paid and airline shares were in arrears. Jeff borrowed heavily from Citibank against his prized piece of real estate, Brookside.

There was a last-blast black-tie party at Brookside in February, 1991. A snowstorm was blanketing the East and Jeff called to ask if I could pick up George and Jennifer Lang in a limousine to bring them up to Westchester. Suzy Downe was going as my date. George owned the esteemed Café des Artistes, and he brought along two bottles of Dom Perignon with glasses for our trip north to Rye. There were perhaps fifty people, an orchestra, a large buffet. Jeff, who loved to entertain, seemed hyper as he sang along with the orchestra. And then from the bandstand he asked Erin to dance, and she said, "No thank you," and sat there. It was a scene out of The Great Gatsby. It was the end of an era, a marriage, of Brookside. The banks took Brookside, and Jeff was soon out of business. Erin filed for divorce. I, now 65, retired as the company was going down. I had been at East/West for 15 years.

THE FREE LANCE FOLLIES

After working without interruption for 43 years, what do you do when you don't have an office to go to? You shift gears, for sure. I belonged to the New York Athletic Club and went regularly to its fitness rehab center at least three mornings a week. I spent more time in Wainscott. I had sold the Los Angeles house some years before and moved my art work and the best of the furniture east to Wainscott . I was sharing the East 57th street apartment now with Bob Schaeffer. The company had given me the leased Mercedes station wagon and since Bob was working with Reed, the British publishing company with U.S. headquarters across the Hudson River in Secaucus, New Jersey, I encouraged him to use the car to commute. Eventually Bob retired too, and we began to split our time between Wainscott and New York. In 1994, The East Hampton Star, the 100-year-old weekly newspaper that was then the voice of the Hamptons, hired him as senior editor and he had to be full time in the Hamptons house.

I wasn't ready for a lazy retirement and free-lance magazine assignments began to come my way, some that I sought and some that arrived from editors who knew me. Town and Country's Pamela Fiori sent me to Charleston to write an article detailing the effect of the contemporary Yankee Invasion, northerners buying up the plantations and the great houses South of Broad Street of that cradle, not only of the Confederacy, but of cordiality. She also sent me to the superb ski resort of Whistler, British Columbia, site of the 2010 Winter Olympics.

Richard Wurman asked me to edit a guide to Charleston, called C The Charleston Guide, and I bunked for weeks with Ben and Barbara in their Mt. Pleasant house researching it and discovered The Notes, a house-by-house history of every significant dwelling in the city that is a must for every one of the licensed folk who guide visitors around Charleston. It was available to anyone who would pay $20 for it. It is a treasure.

I persuaded Smithsonian to give me an assignment on Peter Chermayeff, the Cambridge-based architect who had perfected the art of designing aquaria--from Boston to Osaka, Baltimore to Chattanooga. That one was a challenge that took a year to research and write under the strictest of editorial guidelines. From how to keep aquatic life healthy in an enclosed tank to how humans can survive at an oxygen-deprived altitude, for American Health I wrote a piece about man and oxygen.

Departures editor Gary Walther gave me a raft of assignments. His magazine was for American Express Platinum card members and everything in it was designed to appeal to the first-class upscale traveler. I did ski pieces for Departures on Aspen, Telluride, the Post Hotel in Lake Louise, the extravagantly decorated hotel Les Airelles in Courchevel. Gary sent me to Santa Fe to drive the great circle of Indian ruins around the Four Corners country, a trip I had always wanted to take, from the Navajo's Canyon de Chelly to Monument Valley, the cliff dwellings of Mesa Verde and the Anasazi ruins of Chaco Canyon. Bob Schaeffer came with me for the spectacular trip.

House Beautiful sent me to Italy's Veneto to write about the 16th century architect, Palladio. Friends from Denver, Tom Nussbaum and Sherry Seaver, joined me in Asolo at the lovely Cipriani hotel and we toured the poppy-filled meadows and the rolling hills of the Veneto, seeking out a dozen 16th Century Palladian creations that are icons of classical architecture, from the Villa Mazur to the Villa Rotunda, from the Palladian bridge at Bassano del Grappa to the Villa Emo. My brother Ben and his wife Barbara were in Padua with an Elder Hostel group, and they joined me in Vicenza for a Monteverdi concert in Palladio's exquisite Teatro Olympico. As the a capello choir voices soared, I counted the marble statues that topped the proscenium arch—there were 100 of them.

The next day, we went to see the Villa Malcontenta and after lunch on the Brenta Canal to visit Villa Cornaro in Pimbino Dese, the double-porticoed and columned Palladian villa that was prototype for two of Charleston's most celebrated dwellings, the Miles Brewton House on King Street and Drayton Hall out near Middleton Place. Thomas Jefferson's first sketch for Monticello was also inspired by it. Since Ben and Barbara live in the Charleston area I knew they would find this villa particularly interesting.

The Villa Cornaro turned out to be more interesting than we expected. It was only open for visitors at 3 p.m. on Saturday afternoons. We waited across from the splendid iron gates until we saw a lady in a denim skirt and tee-shirt come down the steps and open them. She asked in English if we wanted to be guided in English or Italian. She was Sally Gable of Atlanta, Georgia, who with her husband Carl had found the house in an ad in The New York Times Magazine. Carl Gable was on Charleston's Spoleto Festival board. We were the only visitors that afternoon and we had a delightful two hours with Sally Gable as she told us the history of this remarkable dwelling and how they had found and restored it. She has recounted the story in a lovely book, Palladian Days, published by Knopf.

For House Beautiful, I accompanied John Rogers to Bali, its neighbor islands of Lombok and Java, as he supervised the making of Colonial-era style teak furniture and crafted artifacts he imported for his design company. We stayed at the Oberoi in Bali, the Amanusa in the Balinese artist city in the hills at Ubud. In Jogjakarta on the island of Java I visited batik making studios and climbed to the top of the extraordinary 12th Century Buddhist temple complex of Borabadour, the Ankor Wat of Java.

After a career in magazine editing that had taken me to many of the world's fabled destinations, these two House Beautiful trips were journeys to dream of. I had long discovered that traveling with a purpose was much more rewarding than just traveling as a look-and-click tourist. On my ski assignments I was fortunate to get to know the makers and doers, the heads of the stations, and to ski with Olympic-quality skiers.

Two magazines, Snow Country and Ski, gave me many assignments, thanks at first to John Fry, founding editor of Snow Country, whom I had known since my Sports Illustrated ski-editing days, when he was the editor of Ski Magazine. I was sent by Snow Country to do stories on Sun Valley, the remaking of Aspen Highlands, and Colorado's Summit County. I had repeated assignments to Utah, and most notably, to Deer Valley, the resort rated over and over again as the number-one ski resort in the country by Ski Magazine.

I did, for Ski, a profile of Edgar Stern who built Deer Valley. He was the grandson of Julius Rosenwald, head of Sears Roebuck. I became friends with Edgar and his wife Polly and dined with them on every visit in front of the fire in the Mariposa restaurant. Stein Eriksen, ski director of Deer Valley and the Norwegian Olympic champion from 1952 is world famous for his grace on skis. Each time I visited he took me on tours, and skiing behind Stein on the lovely groomed powder of Deer Valley, emulating his feet-together, super angulated style, one felt that it is indeed possible to ski, just once, like Stein. Just Once Like Stein had been the title of a Sports Illustrated photo essay in the early 60s.

For Snow Country I went to Lech in the Austrian Arlberg to profile Emo Heinrich, who for 30 years had been one of the most influential ski school directors in America, teaching thousands at Squaw Valley, Portilllo and Stratton, Vermont. He had returned home and built a bed and breakfast up the hill at Ober Lech. The piece was called Emo's Place. The last time I had been in Lech, after skiing over from St. Anton with photographer Dimitri Kessel, we had been stopped as we entered The Post for lunch. "Please, no pictures of the queen," said the guard. And then there appeared in ski gear Juliana of the Netherlands. The Dutch royal family visited The Post every winter.

The European Ski Commission asked me, season after season, to join a small press contingent to the Alps, and took us over the years to Bormio and Cortina in Italy, Innsbruck in Austria, Klosters, St. Moritz and Pontresina in Switzerland. I continued to be invited on press trips abroad. I never accepted an invitation for such a junket without a magazine or a newspaper assignment to place the story. The French Tourist office took a group of us on a tour of Alsace, from Strasbourg down the wine route to Mulhouse. At the automobile museum in Mulhouse, filled with gleaming models of every Bugatti ever made and 500 other splendid examples of the entire history of auto making, I did a story for Sports Illustrated.

I was asked to go to Sicily by the Italian Food and Wine Commission with a group of restaurant owners from all across America. Tom Passevant, editor of Diversion, a travel magazine for doctors, would gladly publish a story about Sicilian food, and I had a second tour of Sicily after 40 years. This time, the major change I found on that beautiful island was the autostrada that circled it instead of the narrow winding roads I had driven in the '60s with Ruth Lynam. During the decade of the 90's, I wrote 40 articles for a variety of magazines and newspapers. As I approached my 75th birthday and the millennial year 2,000, it was time to take down the free-lance shingle.

HEELS UP IN WAINSCOTT

Mother died in 1997 at the age of 95. Her careful guardianship of her affairs left Burton, Ben and me a comfortable legacy. She had nurtured us for all of her life and now she was giving us security for our futures. With part of my share, we turned the Wainscott house from a simple beach cottage into a permanent and comfortable home. The original had been built as economically as possible 35 years before. At the first remodeling in 1983, when the kitchen was added, the contractor discovered three different brands of insulation in the walls, a sign that the original builder cut corners by using materials from other jobs. But the neighborhood had become increasingly desirable. Each of the 20 houses that either faced or abutted the quiet shady blocks of Roxbury Lane had been remodeled or completely rebuilt since I had bought the house.

Bob and I with Harry Bates, my architect friend in Sag Harbor, began to plan an expansion. Prime goals were to add a great room with lots of glass, bookcases and a fireplace adjoining the existing living room, to add a basement to replace the inconvenience of crawl space, to expand a master bedroom and bath and add a glass-roofed solarium adjoining it, and to replace every window and door

196

with double pane insulation. In Harry Bates' first remodeling, he had covered the house's board-and- batten front façade with tongue-and-groove cedar siding. Board and batten is all right for a little church in the wildwood, but it lessoned the architectural sleekness that was Harry Bates' signature.

Impressed by several restorations that the contractor Wayne Koons had done, we hired him to do the work. While adding 1500 square feet to the existing structure, we completely resheathed and rebuilt the house, from basement to roof. Knowing that we would be bringing furniture out from the soon-to-be-abandoned New York apartment, we made floor plans to accommodate important pieces, such as a Welsh dresser, 18th Century Queen Ann chairs, a long Charles XII settee and a variety of art. We designed the openings, the fenestration around them.

The great room is the focal point of the house today, with a peaked ceiling that soars to 20 or more feet, clerestory windows all around and an enormous triangle of double glass high on one end, looking into the trees. The prized Ellsworth Kelly Green Arch is perfectly placed beneath that window. For the mantle we wanted a rough-hewn old beam, not something Georgian and fancy. Wayne, from his remodeling jobs, had a lot of beams and brought several by but they weren't imposing enough. One morning I was walking our golden retriever, Malcolm, on Gibson's beach with Tony Harvey and his golden, Rufus. Our friend Tony is, by the way, a British film director. He directed The Lion in Winter and other films and lives nearby. As we returned to the beach head, Malcolm ran far ahead and lifted his leg on some driftwood. It was the perfect beam, 10 inches square, aged by the sea and the elements, perhaps 14 feet long. Did it come from a boat or from a barn? Who knows. I told Wayne that I had found our mantle, and he and two helpers went to retrieve it. Cut to fit, installed with steel supports, it became the mantle. Beloved Malcolm died of cancer, only eight years old. There is a brass plaque on the end of the beam that reads, Malcolm's Mantle. 1996-2004.

It took six months to finish the construction, and we were at last in the house by mid-summer. Through the spring, friends nearby who only came out in summer, let us use their house while we watched the day-to-day progress, and we moved back in when the work was half finished. On Labor Day, all was in order, our collection of Navajo rugs on the floors, the New York upholstered pieces around the fireplace, our books, including Bob's hundreds dedicated to the lives of British royals back to Edward the Confessor. I had inherited my great-grandfather Matthews's hand made walnut bed and it went into the guest wing, covered with a quilt that had been stitched over a period of six years by Mother and Grannie.

Wainscott house, sleek exterior and, inside, Malcolm's Mantle

A pair of 19th century ranch chairs made of longhorn cattle horns, a collection of blue and white porcelain on the Welsh dresser, a handsome curly maple desk and chest that had belonged to Bob's great-great-grandfather and a backgammon table Bob had made with colored leather points on top, added style to the eclectic mix.

We like to entertain so we commissioned a large circular dining table of old barn pine, with turned legs, comfortably seating eight. It was painted in sanded layers, green, then blue, to look like the milk-paint furniture of 19th Century New England, worn with the ages. The finished house, furnished with art and things collected over lifetimes, is my idea of what a house should be—a portrait of who you are and have become. On Labor Day, to celebrate the completion, we had a barbecue for all of those who had rebuilt the house, Harry the architect, Wayne the builder and his family, Mike the painter and his wife, carpenters and helpers. We were at home in Wainscott, and I would be happy to live here until my final day.

Permanent residency proves to have layers and layers of advantages. For one thing, you get to know not only your neighbors but a slew of people you never knew just weekending. You get involved. Bob left the Star to work in fundraising with Rebecca Chapman, the Southampton Hospital vice president for philanthropy. I had found Timothy Lewis, a Welshman, a former British Navy chaplain, and the new rector of St. Ann's Episcopal Church in Bridgehampton. He is so compelling a presence that I became a member and attend every Sunday. I work on the St. Ann's annual summer house tour, which raises money for the church's outreach programs. When Rebecca Chapman left the hospital to work for the Peconic Land Trust, both Bob and I were enlisted to do volunteer work. We work on the annual Farms and Fields fundraising parties, lunches or dinners in big old barns or a tent in a vineyard. Burton and Hank Harris came from Louisville to join us for one of these one August.

Sister Burton and her husband Hank Harris visiting in Wainscott

All of this leads to meeting more people who have the same goals—doing good for our beautiful community, trying to hold back the tide of over- development of the glorious open spaces and farmland around us, a place where land meets the sea as harmoniously and as handsomely as anywhere on earth.

Bob is a sort of Mr. Democrat in East Hampton, the town that includes our hamlet of Wainscott. He plays golf from April until October, four or five mornings a week. On Thursday, his foursome includes the town supervisor. He writes the Wainscott column for the East Hampton Press and attends Wainscott's Citizen's Advisory Committee sessions monthly. He has been co-chairman of the East Hampton Democratic committee and also helped found, with the actor Alec Baldwin and Silvia Overby, a PAC, or political action committee, called the East Hampton Conservators. It raises money to support candidates who will help preserve our special place.

Beautiful blonde Christie Brinkley is on the board of the Conservators, and whenever I see her says that I made her career! She was on the swimsuit issue cover three times. Bob is also vice chair of the East Hampton Town Planning Board. All of these activities have advantages—you can feel the impact of your efforts in a small community.

Being involved didn't mean being stuck on the East End of Long Island. One summer we were invited by San Francisco friends, Alvin Karstensen and Gloria Volmeyer, to an Italian villa they had taken near the hill village of San Casciano outside of Florence. It is called Il Pozzino, or "little well," and has been in the family for generations of a Tuscan lady, a painter, married to an American, living in San Francisco for most of the year. She only rents to friends or friends of friends. The delightful house, set in an olive grove and surrounded by fields of poppies, artichokes and rosemary, had beautifully furnished sitting and dining rooms and a loggia and terrace filled with geraniums and lemon trees on the first level, and upstairs, three double bedrooms each with a private bath.

Our dear friend Cathy Dugan who had worked with Bob and Leading Hotels and later with us at East/West joined us as did one of Al's California nieces. I accepted the invitation if they would promise to go to Arezzo to see the Piero della Francescos that I remembered discovering with Ruth Lynam those decades before.

We established a very comfortable regime. Every other day we went on an excursion to Florence or to Tuscan towns all around us. Parking in Florence is so difficult that we took the local bus, from a stop just 300 yards down the road. The trip took only a half hour. We revisited the Uffizi—one could spend days there—the Bargello, and all the churches from Santa Maria Novello to Santa Croce and the Duomo. We had lunches in the country and in Florence or in a favorite trattoria in nearby San Casciano, but dinner was at home, every evening. Alvin and I vied as to which one could best turn out an Italian meal. Since we were not driving the narrow curving roads at night, Chianti flowed.

We had seen the double portrait of the Duke and Duchess of Montefelcro, done by Piero della Francesco, at the Uffizi, his only work in Florence. One night I gave the group a lecture on Piero, born sometime between 1412 and 1420, died on October 14, 1492, the day Columbus discovered America. I had a book by Kenneth Clark, with reproductions of his frescos, and told them what to expect in Arezzo and in Sansepolcro, Piero's native town just a winding road up the hill.

Through the Italian Tourist Office in New York, I had a local Arezzo contact, Andrea Mercanti, assistant to the mayor, who met us on the steps of the Chiesa di San Francisco, scene of Piero's master work, the series called the Legend of the True Cross. The walls behind the altar soared to the ceiling with frescoed panels of indescribable beauty. I had not known before the day we were there that the frescos had only recently been restored at the cost of $10 million, funded by the Banco de Lavoro, over the previous 10 years. Only 30 people at a time could pass into the screened off apse which contained them, and Andrea led us through. I had been stunned in 1959. I was overwhelmed at what we saw now.

After a lunch of pappadelle with cinghalli, or wild boar sauce, on the tilting campo of Arezzo, Andrea sent us off to Sansepolcro to see more Pieros at the town hall, the dramatic Resurrection of Christ, stepping from his tomb while guards slept, and the Madonna della Misericordia. Perhaps naively, I felt that Americans knew nothing of this early Renaissance painter, one of the pivotal creators of perspective, a master of light and of faces that you could not forget, whether of a dying Adam or the Queen of Sheba bowing to King Solomon.

Perhaps one reason he is so little known in the U.S. is that there are only three minor works by Piero in American museums, one of St. John the Apostle at The Frick, a Madonna in Williamstown, a portrait of a standing Hercules at the Gardiner in Boston. So little is known of the life of this man, who never married and stayed close to his home base for most of his creative life that I resolved to try to put some flesh on those ancient artistic bones.

Back home I began to search the internet and ordered books about Piero and his time. I enrolled in evening Italian classes at the Ross School in East Hampton. I collected two shelves of books and dedicated myself, like a graduate student, to learn about Humanism, the Renaissance, the Medici. I had only a peripheral knowledge of the period, but I was fascinated. I began to outline a fictional life of Piero, from boyhood working with his father and brothers in the fields growing guado to turn it into indigo dye, to becoming an apprentice in the atelier of Domenico Veneziano in Florence. A mystery. Why did he never marry? Was he ascetic or was he homosexual? I would not label him either one 500 years after his death. There are only 13 documents that record events in his life, such things as a contract to paint an altar piece, his death certificate. Vasari's Lives of the Artists has him being led in his old age, blinded with cataracts, through the streets of Sansepolcro to stand in front of his Resurrection. One of the soldiers sleeping at the base of the open tomb is thought to be a Piero self portrait as a handsome young man.

Two years later, we leased Il Possino, and asked my brother Ben and Barbara to join Bob and me there for two weeks, with a planned third week on The Piero Trail. Now I knew what I wanted to see—everything that Piero had painted and everything that he might have seen when he was an apprentice in Florence that could have inspired or influenced him, the palaces and villas of the Medici whom he could have known, the streets he walked, the artist quarter where he could have worked, even the district along the Arno where a young visitor to Florence might have hung out in wine bars in the 15th Century.

We went to see things that could have influenced Piero's artistic development: Masaccio's Trinity in the Santa Maria Novello, an early marvel of perspective; his frescoed history of St. Peter in the Brancaccci chapel at the Santa Maria del Carmine; the huge painting of Sir John Hawkwood, the conditiori, on horseback, painted on the wall of the Duomo by Uccello, one of the fathers of perspective. We saw the True Cross Legend frescos by Agnolo Gaddi in the Santa Croce, predating Piero's series in Arezzo. Piero would have known them when he worked in Florence as an apprentice to Domenico Veneziano. He is believed to have helped paint Veneziano's Saint Lucy Altarpiece in the Uffizi, and in fact he may have been the model for the St. John in the tableau.

Not all was Piero research. We spent a day discovering the walled city of Lucca, one of the most beautiful of Tuscan towns and another day in Siena. Bob had to leave us during the second week to return to his work in Wainscott. Ben, Barbara and I drove to the hilltop monastery and church of La Verna, the most sacred of Franciscan places. This is where St. Francis received the stigmata. The head brother took us on a tour and we listened to plain song, chanted by the friars, during one of the many daily rituals in the chapel.

207

We spent two days in Arezzo to introduce Ben and Barbara to the marvels in the St. Francisco church. Andrea Mercanti took us to a raucous hall of a restaurant outside of town where Florentine steaks were broiled in an enormous fireplace. After a night in Sansepolcro, where I visited Piero's family home, still standing after 500 years, we drove over the Apennines on a precipitous switch back road to Urbino. Our hotel had been a 15th Century monastery, brought up to 21st Century comfort. It was on the piazza facing the huge Palazzo Ducale of Federico Montefelcro, patron of Piero. Its enormous splendidly decorated rooms contain the state museum of the Marche and Piero's startling, enigmatic Flagellation of Christ.

From Urbino we drove to Perugia, one of the more beautiful hilltop towns in Umbria, to see Piero's magnificent Sant' Antonio altar piece in the National Gallery of Umbria, and then to Assizi. We had been there before in quieter times. The day we were there one almost drowned in the tourist traffic at the St. Francisco cathedral, but it was worth the trouble to see Giotto's frescoed ceiling, depicting the life of St. Francis, carefully restored after the ruinous earthquake 10 years before. No damage could be seen. And so back home, flying from Rome. I had certainly stuck to my travel ideals—traveling with a mission. This trip, Piero led the way.

I began to work on an imaginary life of Piero, and I wrote each morning for six months. After I had written five chapters and more than 100 pages, I shared the work in progress with several book editors and friends. They all agreed that as a writer of fiction I was no Dan Brown. I couldn't trump up artificial mysteries and cliff hangers like The DaVinci Code. I am better at journalism than fiction. My unfinished manuscript is in a file. But the pursuit of Piero gave me a reason to dig into the Renaissance and increase my already deep love for Italy.

In April, 2005, Bob and I took the Queen Mary II, Cunard's new pride, from New York to England. We were extremely lucky on our crossing. The new nomenclature for a Cunard liner is the name of the dining room you are assigned to. Britannia seated 600 in each of two seatings and is tourist class. We booked in Princess Class. Weeks before the sailing, I had a call from our travel agent saying that Cunard was going to refund a substantial amount of our fare. I asked if it could be applied to an upgrade and yes we could for just a bit more, to Queen's Class, top of the lot. With this came a large cabin with two doors onto a balcony, a sitting area, a bathroom with both shower and Jacuzzi tub, and the best food on the sailing. The difference in Princess and Queen's class, both black-tie-at-dinner restaurants, was that in Queen's you could order anything you desired, on the menu or not. I ordered Dover sole three times.

For the crossing, we were at a table for six and found two most agreeable couples. One couple, Jim and Maria Blakely from San Francisco, had sailed the Queen twice before. Maria had broken an ankle some weeks before, and while healed, walked with a cane and had requested easy-access aboard. Cunard gave them an upgrade to one of the premier suites of the ship, a duplex with a butler, two bedrooms and decks all around. They gave a small cocktail party so that all of us could see what one got for a $25,000 transatlantic crossing.

In London, we rented a flat in Chelsea, recommended by friends from Long Island who take it every year. It had been 20 years since I had been in London and it was at its springtime best, full of flowering trees and daffodils and sunshine. We were a block off the King's Road and found a Partridge's a block away to shop for home-style breakfast and dinners. London is one of the most expensive places on earth, and we took buses and the metro instead of cabs and confined our restaurant eating mostly to lunches. We did all of the old London things, the National Gallery, the National Portrait Gallery, the Changing of the Guards at Buckingham Palace. At the National Gallery I saw another Piero della Francesco masterpiece, the Baptism of Christ, given a pride of place, framed by an arch at the end of a long corridor.

I had never been to the Victoria and Albert, and our first Sunday we went there in the morning and stayed for a delicious roast lamb lunch with a chamber music group playing and families from all over the neighborhood. I was so entranced with the V&A's exhibits that I went back a second time before we left. Our only theater excursion was to Alan Bennett's highly praised play The History Boys across the Thames at the National Theater.

My birthday on the lovely Monet

211

The following spring Bob and I joined Ben and Barbara on a two- week Adriatic cruise from Venice to Dubrovnik and back. We sailed on the Monet, a small but luxurious ship with a Croatian crew that takes 60 passengers when fully booked. There were among the 40 of us more Brits than Americans, a friendly and interesting group. We started with two nights aboard in Venice and stopped at a dozen Adriatic ports. At one of them, a group of us took a van to see the Lipizzaner breeding farm at Lipica in the hills of Slovenia.

Bob, Ben and Barbara with a gentle Lipizzaner mare in Slovenia

In a special paddock there were 40 lovely fat pregnant white mares. They and the stallions are descendants of the famous

Spanish Riding School stables that General George Patton saved from the Russians at the end of World War II.

I had visited Dubrovnik, the World Heritage Site treasure of a city with its Venetian-influenced architecture and polished stone streets many years before when I sailed the Adriatic with Jerry Cooke for a Sports Illustrated story. It had been shelled severely during the recent Bosnian war, with Croatia seceding from Yugoslavia. Ten years after, the only visible marks left of the shelling of the town were the views from the walls that surround the city. Tile roofs on rebuilt structures were a brighter brick color than those that had not been damaged and replaced. Dubrovnik sparkled in the Palm Sunday sun. It was birthday time, Bob on April 3, I on April 5, and Barbara treated us to a festive lunch of grilled fish and lovely Croatian wine at a restaurant overlooking the Adriatic.

I had brought a kit of water colors along for the cruise and made sketches daily of the villages lining the ever changing sea coasts. We were seldom out of sight of land as we cruised the Dalmatian islands. There was a Brit aboard who was doing lovely water colors and he gave me helpful advice about choosing one's palate and mixing colors. I had taken water color painting lessons some summers ago at Guild Hall in East Hampton and had become quite competent, but I hadn't been diligent with the work. When I returned to Wainscott I joined a small group that Pia

213

Lindstrom, daughter of Ingrid Bergman, had organized. We met at various garden sites to sketch and paint. That fall, some of us gathered at Pia's house in Water Mill to make Christmas cards

The next time I painted with any seriousness was the following spring, 2007. We rented a house in Provence in the village of Roussillon, an hour from Avignon. It belongs to Richard McGinnis who had worked at Leading Hotels with Bob and Cathy Dugan and now runs the company's Paris office. We started that journey with a weekend in Paris, staying at l'Hotel de l'Universite on the Left Bank, favorite old Parisian stomping grounds. I had visited Paris so many times in the past that I know it almost as well as I know New York. One thing I had never seen was the Arts et Decoratif Galleries that are a part of the Louvre, so we headed there our first morning and were so delighted with the exhibits that we returned a second time.

There were two highlights of the weekend. First was a splendid dinner at The Bistro de Paris on the rue de Lille, recommended by an old friend, Jean-luc Guiazere. And second was a visit on Sunday afternoon with Olivia de Havilland. She was a very close friend of Bob's Uncle Bob Reynolds, and we called on her on his behalf. We had a scintillating two hours with this last living star of Gone With the Wind in her gated town house near the Bois. She was still beautiful at 90, her carefully coiffed hair completely white, dressed in elegant black and pearls. Her attendant served canapés and Taittinger Champagne. As we sat and chatted, the three of us managed to finish two bottles!

With Bob and the lovely Olivia de Havilland in Paris

Then we were off to Avignon by TGV, a speedy three-hour trip through spring, past the neatly gardened and farmed French countryside. Roussillon is a hilled town set among the wild cliffs that are the source of many shades and colors of ochre. All the buildings and dwellings are painted with the colors of the landscape. The house was a gem, a short walk from the central plaza of the village. It has two stories, two bedrooms and a sleeping loft, two baths, a lovely living room with terrace overlooking the tiled rooftops to the ochre hills beyond.

With introductions to various shop keepers from Richard McGinnis we were soon completely at home. Our favorite discovery was Marie-Pierre le Bris who owns a small epicerie called Au Gout Du Jour. Through her we soon knew everyone. She voluntarily opened a charge account for us, loaned us an indispensable pass to the village parking lot just down the hill, and invited us to a party celebrating the first anniversary of her shop. I bought jars of Herb de Provence from her and salute her whenever I use them to add the flavor of Roussillon to an omelet, a salad or a paillard.

There were three bistros lined up side by side on the main square and we soon found our favorite table in the sun. It was Easter week, and this brought touring families, a parade like something out of Jacque Tati's Mr. Hulot's Holiday. Cathy Dugan joined us for the second week and we lived as we had done in the hills of Florence, taking day trips through the Provencal countryside with lunches in one charming village after another, Apt and Lacoste and Bonnieux, and dinner, most nights back at home. One day we drove to Arles to meet Ben and Barbara who were on a Viking river boat cruise down the Rhone. At Ben's suggestion, we met at the yellow café that Van Gogh had

216

painted, and there they were, off the boat for the day. Lunch was at a wonderful restaurant that they had remembered from a long-ago visit.

Ben, Fred, Cathy Dugan, Bob Schaeffer and Barbara Smith at Van Gogh's café in Arles

Roussillon has an academy for the study of color and its various applications in art, decorations on walls, on fabrics, in the building that had once housed the factory for turning ochre into commercial paint and dyes. I bought jars of powdered ochre and enrolled in classes and learned to make my own tempera and water colors. I painted, with colors I had mixed, the 18th Century buildings of the town, the landscapes from our terrace and a stone bridge built by the

217

Romans that was surrounded by a grove of almond trees in full bloom. We will go back!

While I have slowed down a bit physically and hesitate to throw Euros around when the stock market turns down, I travel in my mind, particularly on winter's evenings, reading those things I should have read long ago or have forgotten. I have coursed through all of Proust, War and Peace, Anna Karenina, Brothers Karamazov, Ulysses, and Jane Austen. A new translation of The Canterbury Tales that had been well reviewed even brought me back to the Chaucer of my graduate school days. I found that I preferred the poetry of the original, Professor Burke Johnson's reading of Chaucerian Middle English echoing through the pages. I am now reading Homer's Iliad and will soon address The Odyssey.

Canio Pavone, who was proprietor of a Sag Harbor book store, gives Italian lessons every Tuesday at his house nearby, and I join with five or six others around his kitchen table, challenged, enlightened, and find myself able to read or stumble through conversation in that beautiful language. To keep alert with the bella lingua, I read the Italian press, Corriere della Sera or La Repubblica, most mornings on the Internet.

And I nurture, feed, care for the two dogs that are a constant joy, Oliver, the blonde English cocker, and K-2, the Lhasa Apso. Oliver was a foundling, seduced into the house from the street one October morning when he was lost or abandoned, bramble tangled and hungry with no visible ID. He was about two, the vets thought. No one claimed him, though we tried to find an owner. He is Oliver Twist, the orphan, the love of the household at perhaps 14, half blind with cataracts and losing his hearing.

K-2 is as cute as a button, but a handfull. We found him at ARF, the Wainscott Animal Rescue Fund, after we lost Malcolm, our golden retriever, to cancer. K-2 was only two when someone left him with ARF and now we know why this little fuzzy charmer was up for adoption. He barks at anything that moves, particularly neighbors' cars, and he has teeth like a piranha. But he jumps into your lap when you are doing The New York Times crossword puzzle and cuddles up purring like a cat. His kennel name was PJ, for pajamas, I guess. He is now K-2, named for the famous peak of his native Nepal and for my favorite make of skis.

Oliver the Spaniel and K-2 the Lhasa Apso

Life is good.

4428913

Made in the USA
Charleston, SC
20 January 2010